Profiles in English
as a Second Language

Profiles in English
as a Second Language

Patrick Griffin
Patricia G. Smith
Lyn Martin

Heinemann
a division of Reed Elsevier Inc.
361 Hanover Street
Portsmouth, NH 03801-3912

Offices and agents throughout the world

Published simultaneously in 2003
in the United States of America by Heinemann
and in Australia by
Robert Andersen & Associates Pty Ltd
433 Wellington Street
Clifton Hill, Victoria, 3068

Library of Congress Cataloging-in-Publication Data

Griffin, Patrick.
  Profiles in English as a second language / Patrick Griffin, Patricia G. Smith, Lyn Martin.
  Includes bibliographical references.
  ISBN 0-325-00659-8 (alk. paper)
  1. English language–Study and teaching–Foreign speakers–Evaluation. 2. Second language acquisition–Evaluation. I. Smith, Patricia G. II. Martin, Lyn (Lynette Frances) III. Title.
PE1128.A2G693 2003
428'.0071–dc22

Typeset by Alice Graphics
Printed by China through Colorcraft Ltd., Hong Kong

Contents

Preface

The English as a Second Language (ESL) profiles are the result of many years of work by Professor Patrick Griffin and his colleagues, as they have focused on assessment as a way of improving the education of students who are learning English as a second or additional language in Australia, USA, Canada, Hong Kong, Vietnam and Africa.

In simple terms, a profile is a scale depicting progress in learning. They are designed to assist teachers, schools and systems with the complex process of assessment, recording and reporting on students' developing competencies and achievements. To learn more about profiling it would help to read *Literacy Profiles in Practice: Toward Authentic Assessment* written by Patrick Griffin, Patricia Smith and Noel Ridge. When teachers began to use the profiles designed for students whose first language is English, it became apparent that children whose mother tongue was not English followed a different pathway in their learning of acquisition of literacy skills. The ESL profiles were developed in workshops with teachers almost 2000 students in order to validate the indicators of performance. The indicators then were scaled statistically, grouped into bands and further moderated by ESL teachers.

ESL Profiles are neither assessment tasks, nor do they provide a model for curriculum development. However, they do provide an ascending scale of achievement on which a student's progress can be charted. The charting of such progress provides a consistent approach to monitoring achievement. This approach can be formal or informal but it must be able to be substantiated either by samples of the student's work or by records made by the teacher.

The levels provided allow for two dimensions of language: growth in the development of English and growth in literacy skills. Some students come to our schools literate in their home language. Some are older students. There may be many variations of these experiences. The bands are designed to reflect what growth may be like, but not expecting students to fit a mould.

Initially, it may not be in the assessment process that teachers may find the profiles most useful. The professional development experience is useful in systems where training may not be available for all teachers. Training teachers to be better observers leads to a clearer approach to planning instruction, assisting student learning, and to mapping the progress of individuals. The communication between teachers may be altered, as they have a common language for describing progress.

Acknowledgments

Profiles in English as a Second Language has been developed at the request of many teachers who were successfully using the Literacy Profiles. They recognized that their ESL learners developed literacy skills in patterns that resulted from previous literacy and language learning experiences. This was not surprising, as a decade earlier, when working for the then Ministry of Education in Victoria, Australia, Patrick Griffin, having been responsible for the development of the Literacy Profiles, was even then aware from his research that non-English speaking background students did not follow the same path of development as native speakers.

A project team was set up and led by Professor Patrick Griffin, now Director of the Assessment Research Center at the University of Melbourne, and Dr Elaine Vine, then at the Royal Melbourne Institute of Technology and now at University of Wellington, New Zealand, together with Dr Lyn Martin, now an associate of the Assessment Research Center, University of Melbourne and John Adams of the State Department of School Education.

Dr Elaine Vine played a key role in the development of the project, being responsible for the overall direction of the workshops. Dr Vine provided the theoretical background and expert linguistic assistance to the participants. She clarified the task for teachers, discussed the progress of the work and synthesized the product into a coherent whole.

Further consultation was provided by Professor Merrill Swain, Ontario Institute for Studies in Education (OISE); Professor Bernard Spolsky, Barr Illan University: Professor Alan Davies, Edinburgh University; Lam Kwok Leung, Education department of Kong Kong; Barry Tomlinson, Assessment and Research Center, University of Melbourne: and Janet Saker, John Ingamells, Garey Large and Kathy Prineas, ESL Officers of the State Department of Education.

Many teachers have continued to contribute to the improvement of the ESL Profiles and so this book is based on information about practice. Indeed, there has been enormous growth in understanding about how these diverse students may be best taught. Dr Patricia Smith's contribution synthesizes the work that is being done in classrooms all over the world by teachers to ensure educational equity and opportunity for ESL students.

There are some special teachers who have contributed to the project. Anne Hammond, Joanne Money and Noel Ridge wrote case studies of children that are inspiring. They show us how they use the profiles as part of their teaching. These cameos are illustrated with examples of students' work and with photographs. There is no better way to learn how to do something than to have a demonstration and then try oneself.

Publisher, Robert Andersen has always been an enthusiastic supporter of this publication. Editor Neil Conning and designer Lauren Statham have made sense of visions. Anne Hammond, in particular, has been a photographer whose shots are windows to classrooms.

Chapter 1

Introducing profiles

The English as a Second Language profiles

The ESL profiles provide a means for teachers to report on the growth in English and literacy skills of non-English-speaking background (NESB) students. ESL learners are defined as students beginning school with little or no exposure to English, or perhaps born to parents with language backgrounds other than English. Some are students with no previous formal schooling in any country or students with severely interrupted educational backgrounds. Sometimes they have started school in their new country with schooling equivalent to that which their chronological peers have had in English. Others do not have this start.

In simple terms, profiles are developmental scales depicting progress in learning. They are designed to assist teachers, schools and systems with the complex process of assessment, recording and reporting on students' developing competencies and achievements. They are criterion-referenced interpretive frameworks and are sometimes called standards-referenced frameworks.

An essential feature of a student's profile is that it shows growth. Through its ordered sequence of bands, the profile makes explicit what it means to progress or develop in learning. It provides a framework within which evidence of an individual's progress can be charted and achievements of a school or even an education system can be monitored.

How were they developed?

The predecessors of the ESL profiles, and then the ESL profiles, were developed by observing and recording students in classrooms as they developed their skills and proficiency in English. Teacher observation and judgment were an important part of this process. This practice was based on an understanding that teachers continuously observe and interact with students throughout the school day. As such, they are a rich source of information about student learning, change and progress. All that was needed was a way of explaining the change and communicating this change. This required a common language for the teachers so they could communicate with each other and describe the students' language and literacy behavior. A standards-referenced framework, or a profile, provides both the interpretive framework and the common language.

Teachers assess students continuously and intuitively by observation, interaction, questioning, directing, evaluating and supporting students in the process of learning. This formative, analytical and intuitive assessment is one of the most powerful influences in promoting students' educational growth and development. This source of data has great potential because teachers are enabled to start instruction from where the students are currently most likely to learn rather than where they are meant to be. This constructivist approach helps both teachers and students to develop their language and literacy skills.

There are obviously a large number of approaches to assessing student learning. Any one of the many methods of assessment provides evidence or an observable behavior that can be used as an indicator of learning. However, each on its own provides only a small part of the overall picture. The information a teacher collects through observation on one occasion, or that a test provides on a given day, may be considered as **necessary** information to conclude that learning has occurred, but it may not be **sufficient**. The information may be **appropriate** to the circumstances in which the learning is taking place but it may not be **adequate** for other audiences, such as for the teacher to generalize beyond the classroom. Information must be both necessary and sufficient as well as appropriate and adequate to conclude that progress in learning is occurring and that the skills are generalizable as language proficiency.

By harnessing and formalizing the wealth of information incorporated in teacher observation and intuition and by using commonly shared ways of interpreting, recording and communicating information, the relevant audiences for the teachers' reports (i.e. students, parents, other teachers, school administrators, systems, employers and the community) can be informed about students' established attainment and developing language and literacy. Moreover, the combination of multiple observations from both formal and informal methods of assessment in the form of profiles can provide a more comprehensive view of student performance and developing competence, and adds to the validity of teachers' inferences about student development.

Thus the major aim driving the development of the profiles has been to make both the formal assessment practices (standardized tests and related assessment tasks) as well as the teachers' informal assessment practices (implicit, intuitive and formative) explicit and available to others, so that this increased range of information could be systematically gathered, recorded and communicated and used to help teachers and students. Profiles aim to use teachers' language and assessment practices and to provide teachers with both practical and comprehensive competence indicators. While traditional assessment procedures such as standardized tests may be used to inform and assist teachers, no single test, or sometimes even a battery of tests alone, is sufficient to capture all the explicit or implicit criteria entailed by the notion of *developing competence*. Profiles include the teacher's and sometimes even the students' own evidence and help teachers synthesize these observations within an appropriate framework.

Further development of the ESL profiles

When teachers began to use the Literacy Profiles (Griffin, Smith and Ridge 2000) that were designed for students whose first language was English, it became apparent that children whose mother tongue was not English followed a different pathway in their developmental learning and acquisition of literacy skills. The ESL profiles were developed by working with almost 200 teachers and 2000 students to identify and document the indicators of language and literacy development. The indicators were developed in small groups by expert ESL teachers in workshops. They were then validated by ESL specialists and other teachers before being used in observation checklists to gather data on a large and representative sample of second language learners. Once these data were gathered, the indicators were scaled statistically, grouped into bands and further moderated by ESL teachers and field trials of a range of assessment practices.

ESL profiles are neither assessment tasks nor a model for curriculum development. However, they do provide an ascending scale of development and achievement on which a student's progress can be charted. Charting student progress with the profile indicators can provide a consistent approach for teachers in monitoring achievement. This approach can be formal or informal but it must be able to be substantiated either by samples of students' work or by records made by teachers.

This form of monitoring is quite natural in the classroom. Teachers constantly monitor student progress in a variety of ways. Intuitive as well as systematic monitoring informs their teaching and enables them to define and describe student development and progress. Teaching approaches used for individual students always depend on the formal and informal diagnoses made by the teacher.

Needs of ESL Students

ESL students have more to learn than the native-speaking students when they begin school in an English-speaking community. Some do not even have a concept that a language other than their own exists. Others may be literate in another or even in several other languages but if the scripts are different they must learn a new script. What they all have in common is that they are all learning to understand and speak in English.

A glance at the indicators developed for the profiles is testimony to the work of an ESL teacher. If the students cannot yet speak English, communication can take place in other ways — through drawing, through repeated copying of what has been understood and/or through other non-verbal means. As vocabulary and structure are gradually acquired an inter language begins to develop that approximates English more and more closely if given sympathetic and skillful teaching. All ESL teachers hope that this development occurs and that 'fossilization' does not occur.

The profiles have been written in such a way that they form three separate scales. Listening and Speaking are combined into a single scale and separate scales have been developed for each of Reading and Writing. The number of bands in each scale represents the ESL teachers' emphasis on the pre-eminence of the listening and speaking modes. In addition, the reading and writing modes make allowance for those students who are beginning in their English literacy development and those who are literate in another language.

Profiles of reading and writing in ESL need to deal with two dimensions of language growth in the ESL student: growth in the development of English and growth in general literacy skills. It is difficult to show these two dimensions on a single profile in such a way that that it also accommodates students who enter the educational system at different ages.

Many students enter an English language school system with a level of literacy and with school experiences in their first language that is consistent with their age group in the English-speaking group. However, lower elementary students will have different understandings about literacy from older students and some accommodation is needed for these students. In addition, some students commence school without basic literacy in their first language. These students are described as pre-literate in English as a second language.

Because of their stage of development in literacy, lower elementary and pre-literate students seem to follow different pathways in developing English literacy from those students who are already literate in their first language. Both the lower elementary and the pre-literate student groups are developing separate initial reading and writing profiles from the main group of student ESL profiles. The main ESL Literacy Profile scales cater for students who have well-established literacy concepts in their own language.

Describing the ESL Profiles

The three levels provided for students who have not yet developed literacy skills (The pre-literacy stream A, B and C) include an emphasis on the development of a general understanding of reading and writing. Students who are best described initially in the pre-literacy stream will move on to the reading and writing profiles once they developed basic reading and writing skills in English. Where the students mesh with the general reading and writing scales will depend on their age and how quickly they develop the basic literacy skills.

A schematic model is shown below to show how the pre-literate student's profile links into the main ESL profile scale. The cells labeled A, B and C represent band descriptions of pre-literate mother tongue students' development in English writing. The boxes labeled 1 through 6 represent the development of literate mother tongue students. The transition from one scale to the other is represented by the arrows.

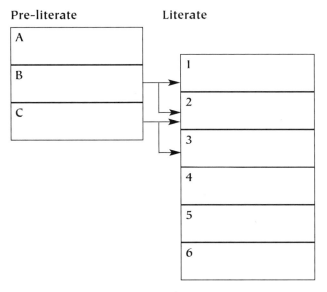

Figure 1.1 Model of the writing scale, illustrating the links between the scales for the mother tongue pre-literate and literate

Profiles are provided to teachers with two facing pages that are meant to be used at the same time. On the right hand page are the indicators and a summary of the outcomes statements at the appropriate level together with advice on how to use the assessment information. On the left hand page is a detailed statement of outcomes applicable to the level together with the preceding and the next level. As students' language development does not fit neatly into one band level (just as it is unlikely to be ever adequately represented by one numerical test score) the profiles allow the development to be described over multiple levels with an emphasis on one level. **Students are placed at the level at which they are showing the most evidence of progress.**

Examples of assessment contexts are provided in this book as suggestions of some procedures to follow to assist the teacher. Teaching strategies are also provided. Record-keeping and reporting procedures are also suggested as well as advice on using the reporting software that accompanies the profiles. The profiles and the software should assist teachers in their

reporting to parents as in assessing the readiness of students to fit into the mainstream classes. Whilst ESL teachers are intuitively aware of this, the profiles provide a useful framework for interpreting observations of students' language development and for organizing descriptions of their achievement.

10 Good Things about Profiles

1. Profiles are holistic. Because they incorporate many kinds of learning, they allow communication of the widest span of learning outcomes: the cognitive, affective, aesthetic and practical.

2. The focus of profiles is to demonstrate competence, regardless of how it has been acquired, rather than to detail course content or be instruments of measurement. This can be across subjects and contexts, in school or at home. It does not relate to the nature of the curriculum or to the content of the texts, reading materials or the process being taught. Experience with the literacy profiles in three countries with widely varying curricula attest to their robustness in this regard.

3. The distinctive feature of profiles is that what is to be achieved is described explicitly. For example, in the scales for writing and reading an extensive range of achievement from early stages to mastery is shown regardless of how that achievement has been assessed or learnt, or of the curriculum in which the learning took place.

4. They include higher order outcomes of knowledge and skills. There is an attempt to go beyond the variations of the curriculum delivered in classrooms and to describe those things that are important for all students to know and be able to do, regardless of the details of the program that they pursue.

5. Profiles allow for a wide range of both formal methods of student assessment (tests and related assessment tasks) and informal methods (observations and descriptive judgments), typically used by teachers to be calibrated and mapped onto a common developmental scale. Using recent developments in item response theory (IRT), the major advantage of the scales is that they make it possible for students' performances on different tasks to be compared reliably — from student to student and from year to year.

6. Profiles provide a framework for the interpretation and communication of the huge amount of assessment information available to teachers — a way of synthesizing teachers' judgments of a wide array of formal and informal assessments. They are particularly useful for interpreting performance assessment and portfolios.

7. Profiles can serve both formative and summative functions. The process of compiling profile data can be of formative use in that it may help the teaching and learning process; the product can serve summative requirements by providing overall indices of achievement for a student or group of students.
8. Profiles are often treated as qualitative, but can have quantitative components. Where there are quantitative components, data may be aggregated across subjects and/or students.
9. The interpretation of profiles is primarily criterion-referenced, but norm-referenced interpretation is sometimes also possible.

Moderation, or teacher comparison of evidence and justification of judgments, is central to the application of profiling. This in turn has implications for both formal and informal professional development of teachers.
10. Profiles may be motivating for students, since motivation is enhanced by emphasis on positive achievements and by allocating to the student some degree of responsibility for the compilation of the profile. Teachers may be similarly motivated by the validation profiles give their judgment and by their usefulness in identifying the positive aspects of student learning.

Understanding the organization of profiles

Figure 1.2 highlights the overall structure of a profile scale using the nutshell statements for writing as an example. Details of the component parts — bands, nutshells and contexts — are presented in later sections that contain the classroom guidelines and materials and show the nutshell statements linked to bands

of development. The nutshell encourages teachers to work first from an overview or holistic approach, focusing on something we call levelness, and then to use the detailed bands as an indicative list of behaviors that signal growth. In short, we work from the nutshell to the detail, and then try to build the profile.

Bands

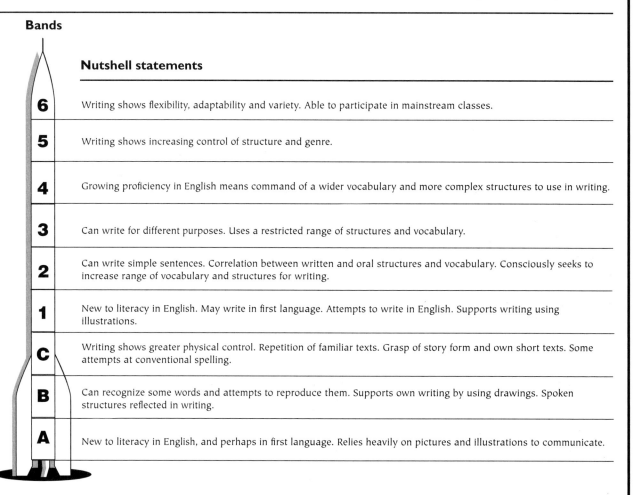

Nutshell statements

Band	Statement
6	Writing shows flexibility, adaptability and variety. Able to participate in mainstream classes.
5	Writing shows increasing control of structure and genre.
4	Growing proficiency in English means command of a wider vocabulary and more complex structures to use in writing.
3	Can write for different purposes. Uses a restricted range of structures and vocabulary.
2	Can write simple sentences. Correlation between written and oral structures and vocabulary. Consciously seeks to increase range of vocabulary and structures for writing.
1	New to literacy in English. May write in first language. Attempts to write in English. Supports writing using illustrations.
C	Writing shows greater physical control. Repetition of familiar texts. Grasp of story form and own short texts. Some attempts at conventional spelling.
B	Can recognize some words and attempts to reproduce them. Supports own writing by using drawings. Spoken structures reflected in writing.
A	New to literacy in English, and perhaps in first language. Relies heavily on pictures and illustrations to communicate.

Figure 1.2 Writing profile rocket

The relationship between the nutshell and the band is shown in the following illustration of one band (band 4) in each of the reading, writing and speaking and listening bands; an example of how the profiles are presented for teachers' use is given on page ••.

Band	Speaking and listening	Reading	Writing
4	**Nutshell statements** Uses English to communicate simple messages. Able to indicate time and tense. Can express simple opinions and ideas.	Able to interpret different sorts of classroom texts. Makes responses to texts. Can recognize word order in familiar texts.	Growing proficiency in English means command of a wider vocabulary and more complex structures to use in writing. Expands vocabulary through many different sources.
	Band statements Can respond to 'Wh' questions in context or to short simple questions. Begins to use 'Wh' question forms, not necessarily accurately. May communicate complex situations using English and non-verbal means. Uses simple English in order to communicate in social situations. Asks what a word means. Uses learned formulaic phrases to meet needs but may not be able to use them correctly in new situations. Has a repertoire of common classroom phrases. Uses the language of play at a basic level. Tries to initiate activities with peers using simple English. Uses some social conventions appropriately. Can express humor and describe feelings.	Chooses to read for interest or to gain specific information. May choose known books from library. Identifies different genres aurally. Reads independently most of the time and with fair understanding. Can read a text for meaning when not all vocabulary is known and be able to identify main points. Interprets maps, graphics and diagrams. Makes a simple critical response to a text or story. Has developed skills in sight organization of discourse, although teacher explanations may be needed for reinforcement. Can read aloud fluently. Pronunciation tends to be correct.	Writes in sentences a short story that has a beginning, a middle and an end. Redrafts a piece of writing after a writing conference. Makes corrections to own writing after rereading. Shows an awareness of purpose and audience in choice of vocabulary and style. Uses consistent verb sense. Uses writing to argue, convince or justify. Can write simple descriptions, recounts and procedural text. Works independently when writing but asks for help if needed. Uses a variety of strategies to check spelling. Uses commas to separate items in a list. Can use simple past and future tenses where appropriate. Can use articles correctly. May show confusion over conjunctions and tenses. Uses appropriate verb forms in response to a question that models the form.

Reading profile record

Profiles are organized in a specific way in this book. The bands are collected in pages that present three bands. This has been done because, in our experience with the profiles, it is common for a class to be spread over three or four bands, and for any individual student to exhibit behaviors described by indicators from within several adjacent bands. Hence, the profile record sheet becomes a recording procedure for teachers. The record sheets are presented as blackline masters and teachers are encouraged to copy them, mark them with highlighter pen and store them in students' portfolios. These profiles and their bands have been in use for some years and have had considerable uptake. Performance data has been collected for these scales.

The next section of the book first describes how to use the profiles and then presents the profile scales together with suggested authentic assessment contexts to use in the classroom.

The third section presents information on recording and reporting to a range of audiences, and shows how the scales may be used for students in a reading classroom.

In Appendix III, a set of blackline masters is presented to enable teachers and administrators to make records and to adapt for reporting purposes. These blackline masters replicate the forms that are produced by the ALPS–ESL software and can be used where the software is not being implemented.

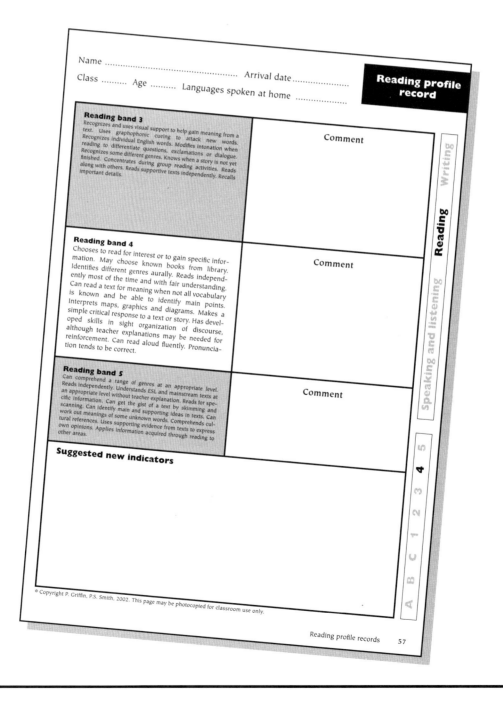

Name .... Arrival date.....................

Class .... Age .... Languages spoken at home ....

Reading profile record

Reading band 3
Recognizes and uses visual support to help gain meaning from a text. Uses graphophonic cueing to attack new words. Recognizes individual English words. Modifies intonation when reading to differentiate questions, exclamations or dialogue. Recognizes some different genres. Knows when a story is not yet finished. Concentrates during group reading activities. Reads along with others. Reads supportive texts independently. Recalls important details.

Comment

Reading band 4
Chooses to read for interest or to gain specific information. May choose known books from library. Identifies different genres aurally. Reads independently most of the time and with fair understanding. Can read a text for meaning when not all vocabulary is known and be able to identify main points. Interprets maps, graphics and diagrams. Makes a simple critical response to a text or story. Has developed skills in sight organization of discourse, although teacher explanations may be needed for reinforcement. Can read aloud fluently. Pronunciation tends to be correct.

Comment

Reading band 5
Can comprehend a range of genres at an appropriate level. Reads independently. Understands ESL and mainstream texts at an appropriate level without teacher explanation. Reads for specific information. Can get the gist of a text by skimming and scanning. Can identify main and supporting ideas in texts. Can work out meanings of some unknown words. Comprehends cultural references. Uses supporting evidence from texts to express own opinions. Applies information acquired through reading to other areas.

Comment

Suggested new indicators

Reading profile records   57

Speaking and listening   Reading   Writing

A B C 1 2 3 4 5

Assessment using profiles

Profiles help teachers to assess and record the development of a student's literacy. They are based on a belief that assessing literacy is an integral aspect of all teaching. Every aspect of a student's classroom work — worksheets, books, listening to them read, or performance tasks — can be considered as an assessment activity.

Treating assessment like this means that the distinction between teaching and assessment becomes blurred. Assessment is integrated into teaching and learning. There is really no need for an end-of-lesson test if the teacher is continuously monitoring the students' work and the students are engaged in rich learning tasks. The records made by the teacher become the most important part of this assessment approach. Profiles help in this regard, but do not constitute all the evidence of the student's learning and development. Portfolios, reading records, reading logs, library records and running records help teachers who use a profiles approach. The profiles help in making an integrated judgment of progress.

Developmental assessment should help teachers to monitor students' growth. Students are asked to do things first that they find easy, and gradually the difficulty of the tasks is increased. Eventually we find that the student is no longer able to consistently display all the evidence described in the profiles. Then, as we look for evidence at even higher levels, there is less and less of the profiles that the student is able to demonstrate.

This leads us normally to conclude that we have found the student's level of achievement. But this is not strictly correct. There are three regions of development that we can identify clearly. The first is the profile level that the student has mastered or that they can demonstrate easily. The second is the set of levels or indicators that the student has difficulty with, but can show some development. The third represents those levels on the profiles that the student has not yet reached.

The second region is especially important. This is the region of intervention for the teacher. Once we know what the student is capable of doing consistently, and what the student is not yet capable of doing, we can concentrate on the region in between, and provide instruction at those levels. It is in this region of development that we find the point of intervention where the student is **ready to learn**.

This is an important way of thinking about developmental assessment approaches such as profiles. The level reached in a personal developmental continuum is not the level of achievement or the end point. It represents the point of intervention for the teacher and where the student is ready to learn. It is a starting point, not an end point.

This conclusion comes from a measurement theory that allows us to directly compare the ability of the student with the difficulty of the tasks they are asked to perform. When the student's ability is exactly equal to the difficulty of the task, the chance of success by the student is 50 per cent. It cannot be considered as a level of achievement, but it is the point at which the student is most likely to develop or learn the skills and underpinning knowledge involved. Mastery and competence are found at levels where the chance of success is higher, or where tasks or behaviors are easier.

The nice thing about this way of interpreting developmental assessments is that every student has a point of intervention and the teacher can find a level at which every student is ready to learn. This way of interpreting is only applicable in a developmental assessment framework. Profiles, as a developmental assessment framework, help to identify the intervention point where student is ready to learn.

In this way the profiles firmly link assessment and teaching. As teaching traces the student's development, every teaching and learning task becomes an assessment task. Each needs to be recorded in a portfolio, a log or a running record. As this is accumulated, the teacher needs to identify the point at which the student is struggling to develop, rather than the point where the work is too difficult. This is the point at which the learner is ready to learn or the teacher needs to intervene. It is also the point on the profiles where we can record the student's development.

This approach can therefore use a possible interpretation of test scores and apply it to profiles. However, test users hardly ever have the opportunity to interpret their data this way. A test score, from a properly developed test, is not an achievement score at all. If it is interpreted on a developmental continuum, the score indicates the point of intervention and the student's readiness to learn. However, few tests of reading, writing or spoken language are, or can be, interpreted this way.

Profiles are one of the first sources of advice for teachers in this method of interpreting assessment advice. No other assessment framework currently takes this approach. Profiles therefore offer unique assistance to teachers.

Impact of the ESL profiles

Teachers are often nervous about the amount of time required to implement profiles. Traditional methods of teaching and assessment are difficult to replace. Holistic, professional judgment approaches to assessment are novel, at least in a sanctioned way. Often, teachers' variable understanding of standards and variation in portfolio interpretation can be linked to personal preferences in teaching and assessment. High-stakes environments render the use of professional judgment approaches to assessment for accountability purposes somewhat problematic. Testing is likely to remain in this environment as the major approach to assessment for monitoring purposes. But teachers need to start somewhere to take control of the assessment agenda. After all, the most powerful source of information about student learning is the teacher. The constant interaction, observation and analysis that occurs in the classroom only needs direction and framing to become a means of monitoring student progress.

But initially, it may not be in assessment that teachers find the profiles so useful. The professional development experience of teachers in all countries using the scales is instructive and, in a way, encouraging for teacher development in systems where training may not be available for all teachers. Training teachers to be better observers of children's learning leads to better learning. It leads to a clearer approach to planning instruction, assisting student learning and to mapping the progress of individuals.

It is in this area that the profiles will have the biggest payoff with mainstream teachers. The communication between teachers is generally altered by the content of the scales. Through staff room discussions, teachers resolve to try new approaches, collect samples of student work to show their colleagues, discuss their ratings of the work and their placement of students on the scales. This points to the important contribution the scales make to the professional development of the teachers. They provide a common language for describing progress. They give the teachers the meta language of proficiency development in English language. Discussions in terms of grade equivalents, of test scores or percentile ranks, stanines or scales cores provide little meaningful information for teachers. The direct interpretation in terms of achievements, competencies and skills observed within a developmental framework provide clearer data. The scales can be translated into other languages for reporting purposes.

Making your rocket set and class record

You can use profiles to report on your class. When you have completed individual rockets for your class, photocopy the class record pages. Shade in the bands on the rocket that correspond with those which your students have completed since you first put them on the bands. You can use different colors for each term. Shade in the individual areas on the class record. It can be assumed that they have completed earlier bands previously. This will let you see at a glance what to report for individuals and on the class.

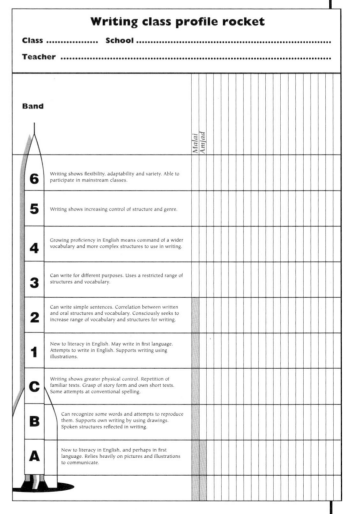

Figure 1.3 Example of rocket and class record

Chapter 2

Learning to use the ESL profiles

Teachers are encouraged to spend time initially to become familiar with the content of the profiles. This is the most important training possible. There is no alternative but to read the profiles thoroughly. The language should be familiar because the indicators were written by teachers experienced in ESL classes. Samples of students' work are used to locate the appropriate level for instructional and reporting purposes. With older students, self-assessments can also be used, but it is advisable to begin this two to three weeks before the data will be used for a full assessment so that the student self-assessment is based on a proper approach, consistent with the profile. Self-assessment itself can be a powerful learning experience for students.

Getting to know how to use the profiles

Read through all the profile bands. Think about a particular student.

Let's think about Ruiz. Examine the samples of his work that you have already collected and analyzed. Look at the nutshell statements. Which one best describes this student? Now you can match the work to the bands.

Assessment contexts appear on the left-hand page opposite the bands. These will help you gather evidence of the student's progress and create situations for observing the student's activity. They will help you know what to look for when analyzing progress.

Now that you are more confident and familiar with the bands, you can begin to build Ruiz' profile. To do this, you will look for those indicators he demonstrates regularly that he has mastered. Mark these with a highlighter pen.

He will probably demonstrate indicators in two or three bands. There will be one band in which he is mainly showing progress.

Select another two or three students, perhaps one performing better than Ruiz and one who is just beginning to learn English. Repeat the process for them, beginning to build their profiles.

Now that you are comfortable using the profiles, plan how to monitor every student to eventually create profiles for each. You will be monitoring the progress of the class and of each student.

Place all the students on the bands (use the photo-copiable blackline masters in Appendix III) and keep them in a folder or on a clipboard in alphabetical order for easy reference.

Each day, select a manageable number of students – no more than three – and observe them in various contexts, make notes about them and collect appropriate written work.

At the end of the week, make a formal judgment about each student using your records and their work samples and transfer this to their profile by highlighting relevant outcomes.

Use a highlighter pen to mark those indicators regularly demonstrated. Check regularly through the student's work for further evidence. Talk to anyone else who has contact with the student.

Gathering the information

Profiles are very useful for providing teachers with a road map or pathway so that they can see what the students have done, and then plan for their learning individually, in a group or as a class. Information needs to be gathered about learning through observing and collecting samples of students' work. The profile nutshell statements and bands can be used to interpret learning. This means that all teachers will be using similar statements to describe learning.

The teachers first plan and collect resources for a lesson.

Reading a story is a context for observation. Certain responses may be noted.

If the story has repetition as in:
'Run, run as fast as you can.
You can't catch me,
I'm the Gingerbread man.'

The students who join in are demonstrating that 'They repeat modeled utterances of very short phrases with understanding'. This may be highlighted on their individual profile for band 1.

You may notice that several students did not respond to the implicit invitation to join in.

What do you do next?

For example, plan to read more stories with repetition and maybe look for one in the student's home language.

The following examples, or case studies, demonstrate how teachers with very different kinds of students develop their profiles.

1. Malai

Malai is a Thai student who is literate in her own language. She is 10 years old and a new immigrant attending a language center for the first time. She had been in the English-speaking country for 3 months and in the language center for just 2 weeks when the first writing language sample was collected and assessed. Before attending the language center she spoke no English at all. The translation of the first language text is courtesy of her teacher.

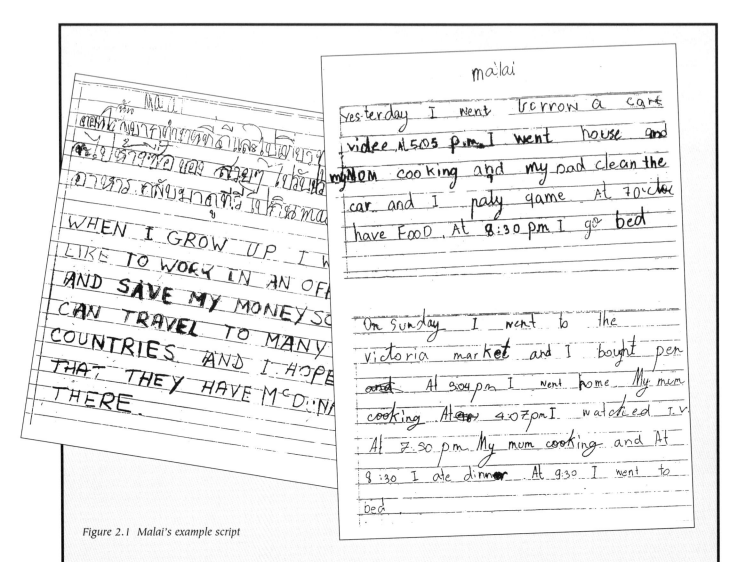

Figure 2.1 Malai's example script

Malai's work presents us with some interesting patterns. The first sample was collected after 2 weeks in the center. She started to write in English very quickly, but the stories were all the same. She used repetitious and formulaic language. Her strategy was to build up a set of acceptable language chunks that she worked into all her stories and repeated until she got it correct or to her personal satisfaction. While this may be the basis of process writing, in this case it can give a misleading impression of her command of the language. Her writing may appear better that it is in reality. The teacher's opinion helped establish her writing level based on this and several other examples of her work. Her attention to detail finds her repeating text in her script in an attempt to get it right. In fact, the teacher reported that Malai would not put the work down until she was satisfied that it was fully correct. To help her in her quest for perfection Malai uses stereotypical language but the sample text here helps to make it clear that she does not yet have control of the past tense.

After four weeks another series of scripts was collected and rated using the profile scales. Now the past tense had emerged somewhat more strongly but the same patterns of language are evident. The teacher's report of Malai's work on the scales is as follows. An examination of the first set of band scales helps to place Malai on the scales. She was placed at band 2. Her teacher's report is also reproduced for information here.

Band 2 Possible assessment contexts

- Class shared writing activities, e.g. finishing off a sentence writing a story.
- Word games using dictionaries, word banks to extend and reinforce vocabulary.
- Sentence building exercises.
- Writing two or three simple sentences about self/neighbour.
- Class writing of simple text about excursion.
- Writing a simple shopping list, list of domestic animals, postcard to a friend, simple greeting cards.
- Writing simple dictations.

ESL writing profiles

	Comment
Writing band 1 May initially write in first language. Draws pictures that relate to an ongoing activity or to tell a story. Draws to support a text. Writes own name in full. Completes short sentences with personal information. Completes simple, repetitive modeled sentences. Can copy a sentence scribed by teacher from own dictation. Copies words, labels, signs from the board, books or charts to use in own writing. Copies text correctly from the board or a book. Uses appropriate size, spacing, and letter formation. Is aware of some English sound–symbol relationships.	Comment
Writing band 2 Writes or completes simple sentences from own experiences. May write familiar texts repeatedly, based on modeled repetitive structures. Matches written structures and vocabulary to spoken structures and vocabulary. May use 'and', 'then', 'next' to link ideas in a sentence. Can use repetition and choose vocabulary to add emphasis. Asks the names of things in English to use in own writing. Finds words in charts, books and word banks to use in writing. Can maintain own word banks and topic lists. Finds words from word lists and simple dictionaries. Understands some of the terminology of writing. May use some punctuation to break up ideas. Knows that sentences start with a capital letter. Attempts to spell some new words using knowledge of English graphophonic conventions. Asks for the spelling of words to use in own writing. Contributes ideas, sentences or words to a class or group story.	Comment
Writing band 3 Uses a known story form to begin writing. May borrow structures from well-known stories to write own stories. Chooses own topic to write about. Can write a few lines on a topic of interest that has been covered in class. Can write short, factual text independently. Writes own simple journal or diary entries independently. Can write several sentences with connected ideas. Refers back using pronouns. Uses connectives such as 'and', 'but', 'because' to link ideas in short texts. Structures used in writing such as word order may reflect some first language features. Uses capital letters appropriately for proper nouns. Uses some more complex punctuation. Supported by class discussion and activities such as modeling, can retell a narrative in writing. Can provide an alternative ending for a story. Shares writing with a partner or a group. Can name all the English letters and knows the sounds they commonly represent. Can present writing appropriately for different audiences or for display using headings, layout and illustrations. May experiment with lettering.	Comment

Figure 2.2 Writing bands 1 to 3

Teacher's Report: Malai

Malai is very motivated to write and will initiate her own writing in any free time. She is now writing totally in English in the classroom. Her own personal writing is generally in the form of a simple text that communicates events and experiences. She is able to represent an idea in a sentence and is developing punctuation skills to separate ideas. She is able to fulfill a number of purposes using a range of writing media. She can write cards, record new words in her dictionary and use a computer for her final draft.

Malai is writing texts showing a beginning, a middle and an end and her ideas are sequenced logically. Her sentences show subject-verb-object patterns and she is beginning to link sentences with 'and'. She is able to use time indicators and 'went' but generally uses simple present or present continuous tense for her range of tenses. Malai is very concerned about correct spelling and will use her dictionary, teachers or peers as a resource. She is always keen to rewrite after corrections or conferencing. She also tends to use repeated formulae to generate and structure writing and continues to write about the same topic or theme while incorporating new vocabulary items and details.

On balance: Band 2 writing.

Figure 2.3 Malai's report

2. Amjad

Amjad presents us with another example of developing language. At the time of the assessments he was 9 years old and had never been to school neither in the home country nor in his new English-speaking country. The two samples of writing are taken from his work at the beginning of the school year. Amjad writes

> My Name is Amjad,
>
> My school, Lagron Central, is in Scrayville
>
> This is my school.

This is the first piece of writing he ever produced — at least for the teacher. He was given a tick and told it was 'fantastic'. After two weeks Amjad was still using the repetitious patterns but had expanded the vocabulary.

In my house I have a very big cat.

This is a very nice cat.

I am heavy and I am heavy like a bull

This is a nice cat.

This is very easy

My name is Amjad

This is my family

My father's name is Kare

My mother's name is Safen

My aunt's name is Monra

My big brother's name is Ashraf

My sister's name is Shrafa

My small sister's name is Shima

This is my family

Figure 2.4 Amjad's scripts

A quick exploration of the scales lets us see how the student's work is developing. Amjad writes from left to right, using environmental print well. Repetitions are a feature of his language. Upper and lower cases are emerging.

As a strategy, the teacher word processes the materials and gives them back to Amjad for his folio. Amjad's work is an example of what can be used to place the student on the pre-literate stream scales.

Amjad used formulaic language. His command of structure was weak but he was able to communicate in writing on very familiar topics and in a limited way. He used symbols and pictures to accompany his text and attributed simple meaning to the text. He copied words from the environment and used a restricted set of very familiar words. He also copied sentences provided by the teacher. He has attempted to write sentences of his own and contribute his own ideas to the text. The second example shows that after three weeks he progressed from band A to band B on the pre-literate scales but had not yet developed the basics of writing and so could not yet be placed in the mainstream scales.

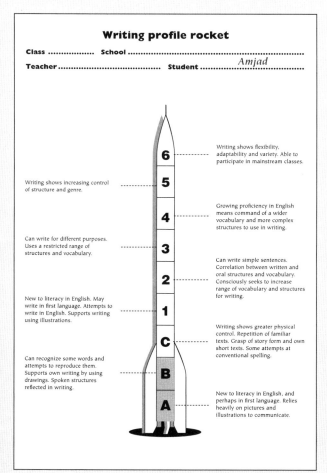

Writing class profile rocket

Class .... School ....
Teacher ....

Band

6	Writing shows flexibility, adaptability and variety. Able to participate in mainstream classes.
5	Writing shows increasing control of structure and genre.
4	Growing proficiency in English means command of a wider vocabulary and more complex structures to use in writing.
3	Can write for different purposes. Uses a restricted range of structures and vocabulary.
2	Can write simple sentences. Correlation between written and oral structures and vocabulary. Consciously seeks to increase range of vocabulary and structures for writing.
1	New to literacy in English. May write in first language. Attempts to write in English. Supports writing using illustrations.
C	Writing shows greater physical control. Repetition of familiar texts. Grasp of story form and own short texts. Some attempts at conventional spelling.
B	Can recognize some words and attempts to reproduce them. Supports own writing by using drawings. Spoken structures reflected in writing.
A	New to literacy in English, and perhaps in first language. Relies heavily on pictures and illustrations to communicate.

3. Eman goes to school

This case study is about planning to meet the needs of young children in a multicultural classroom. The children are from culturally and linguistically diverse backgrounds who are learning English as a second or additional language. It addresses the issue by focusing on Eman, a five-year-old girl from a Turkish family, but keeps in mind that a multicultural perspective would reflect the language and cultural diversity of all students in the class. Eman, like the others, brings with her a rich diversity of life, family and other experiences that need to be respected and valued by her teacher.

Eman was born in Australia. Her parents, Fatma and Mohommed, were born in Turkey and their two families migrated separately to give their children a better life. Eman goes shopping with her mother and sees signs in Arabic, Turkish, Italian and Greek describing the shops and their contents. She is quietly social and responds, 'Bon giorno, Senora' to Sophia in the pharmaceria and, 'Kalimera, kirie Nick' to Nick as he arranges his new tomato display in front of a sign in Greek and in English. She waits and listens as Fatma selects a good chicken in the halal butcher's. At the sweet shop there is a discussion about whether to get Turkish delight or baklava for the expected visitors. A gift of a sweet elicits a shy smile and a quiet 'Thank you, Mrs ...'. When the shopping is unpacked at home Eman can see labels in two or three languages. She is surrounded by print and knows already about how language and literacy can be used.

Developing a multicultural perspective

The idea of developing a multicultural perspective in a classroom is much broader than teaching children English. Such a perspective recognizes the similarities and differences in children and builds on the cultural and linguistic diversity within the class. By reflecting cultural and linguistic diversity in the program, the children learn that there are many ways to do things. They learn that languages are just 'different', not 'foreign', and a positive attitude towards others comes about. Eman's teacher has learned greetings and other practical words in Turkish and the other home languages of the children in her class provide a role model for all the children in the group. She figures that if a five-year-old can operate comfortably in a multilingual society, she should be able to learn such basics, too. So she greets Eman in the morning, 'Salaam aleikem, Eman' and Eman responds, 'Aleikem salaam, Lisa'.

Parent participation

A multicultural perspective permeates all aspects of the day, including the day-to-day reading, writing and other experiences and the work with parents and the wider community. Multiculturalism is not something that happens in response to festivals or as part of theme, such as 'Spanish week' or 'International day' though, of course, these should be part of what happens. In particular, they provide a platform to encourage parent participation. The best resources are the family themselves. Families can provide a wealth of information and assistance to help the teacher develop a perspective that is based on what families themselves think is important. Families can help as a language support and are a resource for stories, photos, artifacts as well as food and festival information. This use of families as a resource helps them feel comfortable in coming into the school and help them take an active role in their child's education.

The school has deliberately set out to make the parents welcome. A small room has been painted and furnished as a tea and coffee room to encourage the mothers especially to feel comfortable at school. An adult ESL class also operates in the school. Many women find this easier than traveling into the Adult Language Center and the attendance rate is almost 100 per cent. Multilingual notices are used and this sends positive messages to parents that their language is valued and that the school welcomes families from diverse cultural and linguistic backgrounds. The inclusion of parents in the program also demonstrates that the parents' cultural, linguistic and religious backgrounds are valued and seen as positive assets. It is important to offer parents a range of options for involvement that are meaningful and comfortable. Eman's mother assists by helping to maintain the Turkish children's first language by reading stories, often from Eman's own books, singing songs, cooking, interpreting for other parents on issues that are not confidential, and supporting new parents in the enrolment process.

First and second language acquisition

The classroom is a very rich environment for supporting language development because many opportunities are provided for the children to interact with others. It is a bonus if this talk takes place in the first language as well as English. The children have probably come to school having begun to learn their second language. The teacher should encourage keeping the first language strong because family ties are maintained, strong foundations for later learning are made and also the advantages in life of bilingual communication.

Learning English — the print walk

How can the teacher begin to use what Eman already knows about English and about literacy when she comes to school? The teacher knows that Eman, and the other children go shopping with their mothers. So she plans to take the class on a print walk.

The children are excited. They begin the print walk by stopping at the main entrance of the school. 'There is the sign that tells people the name of our school. Can you read it with me?' asks the teacher, deliberately giving them the clues they need to successfully read the sign.

'Well done, everyone! You read that beautifully', she says. The children become excited as they walk towards the busy shopping center, reading many signs along the way.

Van calls out 'STOP!' as we approach a stop sign.

'That's great reading, Van.'

They stop outside the Lebanese bakery. The teenager behind the counter smiles and waves. They wave back. Eman and some others call out, 'Salaam Aleikem, Nilvan.' They have been here before.

There are many words painted on the window some in Arabic and some in English. 'Can we find the words "hot bread"? What letters do "hot" and "bread" start with?'

Kim knows her letter sounds well and calls out enthusiastically, 'H for hot! B R for bread!'

'I found it! I found it!' Eman points to the words.

We read 'Hot bread' together.

'Here it is, too.' Eman points to the Arabic and Joe agrees with her.

The children continue their walk. They are surprised and delighted to discover that they are able to read many signs in their environment, including those in other languages. The teacher finds that there are enough clues for her to negotiate her way successfully and the children are pleased she is able to read so much. They learn that she uses clues to make meaning because she tells them what she is doing. 'I think that must be the word for chemist shop because that is where the name would be, just in front of the chemist's name.' The excursion provides a rich basis for talk, reading and writing in the classroom for the next week.

Learning English — reading books

Eman's teacher has found out that she really loves books. Fatma brings in some photos of her daughter reading with her aunt, her father, her mother and by herself. She explains that they bought books in English as well as in Turkish. They wanted their daughter to be able to read comfortably in both languages. They themselves do not move so well between the two languages because their parents had wanted them to become good at English and had not encouraged reading and writing in Turkish. Their parents had not understood that many young children throughout the world successfully learn more than one language from birth. To be bilingual they need to have a good foundation in both languages.

The teacher, with the parents' help, can use bilingual and multicultural notices. The use of bilingual notices sends positive messages to parents and to the children that their home language is valued and that the classroom welcomes families from diverse cultural and linguistic backgrounds. She values all the experiences the children bring to their schooling. The teacher, taking her cue from Eman's parents, is setting up a library of books that reflect diversity and includes books in the languages of the community. She plans her program to effectively meet the needs of the children and doesn't try to use a 'one-size fits all' model.

Learning English — the communicative approach

As we have seen with Eman, children seem to learn languages best without formal instruction. This is called the communicative approach. This approach surrounds children with natural language such as in play, conversations, songs and games, stories and rhymes. Children learn the meaning of words and phrases in real-life situations and they feel confident to use the new language in a relaxed atmosphere. Eman's teacher remembers that she initially responded non-verbally and often used single words to name objects or attract attention or by the use of routine short phrases used regularly during the school day, such as 'come and sit on the mat', 'this is a ...' and 'read with me'.

Introducing the profile scales

The daily observations of Eman and the other children, recorded on individual record forms, provide a basis for placing the children on the ESL Profile Scales. The scales help interpret Eman's progress in common terms. The teacher decides that the nutshell statement for band 3 describes Eman as a speaker and listener:

SPEAKING and LISTENING band 3

Nutshell statement

Communicates simply in English.
Takes part in everyday activities and routines.
Experiments with the structure of English.
Increases knowledge of English by borrowing from other speakers and familiar sources.

The teacher uses a highlighter to show the skills she has observed:

Speaking and listening band 3

Can use own simple constructions. May use simple adjectives to describe or add emphasis. Responds to questions from peers or teachers with a single word or phrase. Makes simple requests to satisfy immediate needs, using non-verbal language as well as simple expressions. May initiate communication in a small group. Borrows key words from previous speaker. Shows confidence in familiar class and school routines by responding appropriately to instructions and asking for some clarification. May use structures and copy stress and intonation patterns from familiar repetitive stories, songs and rhymes. Uses some appropriate terminology when requesting. Demonstrates active listening. Enhances speaking by using a variety of non-verbal conventions. Understands that talk can affect other people.

Because Eman shows all the indicators in band 3 it is very likely she is also developing some band 4 indicators and so the teacher would be conscious that she should be watching for them and also scaffolding Eman's learning for a particular purpose. For example, one suggested activity is to set up group problem solving activities that will give opportunities for students to negotiate meaning with others and report on shared conclusions. This may be organizing a menu for a class afternoon tea and assigning tasks.

Evaluation

This case study has described how programs can be planned effectively to meet the needs of children from a range of cultural and linguistic backgrounds, including children who may be experiencing an English-speaking environment for the first time. The teacher has followed seven steps:

1 Developed a knowledge base
2 Demonstrated a philosophy and policy
3 Gathered and recorded information on individual children
4 Interpreted observations and set aims
5 Planned strategies
6 Implemented plans
7 Evaluated

The evaluation step is essential because it provides a basis for future planning. The daily content, the organization of space and time, the provision of both flexible and predictable contexts and how the teacher and others work within the program can all be evaluated. This ensures a responsive and stimulating program for the students.

4. Xiao Yan in New York

Xiao Yan is a Chinese-speaking child in Jessica's kindergarten classroom. Her family moved to New York from Shanghai when Xiao Yan was three years old. The family shares an apartment in Lower Manhattan with her maternal grandmother who is Chinese. Her mother, who had been a teacher for 15 years in Shanghai, has very little English. She is employed in a factory where most of the employees communicate in Chinese. Her father is self-employed in a cleaning business and is able to communicate fairly successfully in English. Her grandmother often brings her to and from school. Discussions between the family and school are conducted with the father who acts in the role of interpreter for the mother when she is able to attend.

Xiao Yan settled quickly into the kindergarten classroom. She immediately formed an attachment to Jessica, responding to her welcoming manner and to the well-organized and structured classroom program.

During the first semester, Xiao Yan developed in confidence. She responded well to classroom routines, clearly recognizing and managing her materials, responding to directions during whole class or small group meeting times and cooperating socially with other students. In whole class situations she responded cheerfully when approached but did not generally offer comment. When visitors came to the classroom, she would often seek them out, asking,

'Who are you?' then inviting them to come and see what she was doing.

Jessica observed her students regularly and acted according to their perceived needs. She ensured that Xiao Yan was given opportunity to participate in group activities such as role-play, drawing or construction, which provided her opportunity for informal social interaction with other students. She noted that during shared reading time Xiao Yan enjoyed joining in with the refrains of familiar tales. Revisiting these books again at the listening center, where she could follow the words more closely while hearing the text read again, helped develop her reading strategies and further her enjoyment of the reading experience. Sometimes she could be heard chanting these refrains during follow-up activities. For example: 'There's a hole in my sock and a hole in my shoe. Oh no!'

Speaking and listening band 4

Can respond to 'Wh' questions in context or to short simple questions. Begins to use 'Wh' question forms, not necessarily accurately. May communicate complex situations using English and non-verbal means. Uses simple English in order to communicate in social situations. Asks what a word means. Uses learned formulaic phrases to meet needs but may not be able to use them correctly in new situations. Has a repertoire of common classroom phrases. Uses the language of play at a basic level. Tries to initiate activities with peers using ·simple English. Uses some social conventions appropriately. Can express humor and describe feelings.

While revisiting the environmental print during a regular class or small group print walk, Jessica observed and recorded that Xiao Yan could recognize her name among others and identify letters from her name in isolation. Very soon she was able to identify a growing list of high frequency words. When Jessica included her in guided reading sessions, Xiao Yan was quick to recognize the repeated pattern of the simple texts and to identify words in isolation, yet appeared to find difficulty in making meaning from her reading. Jessica looked closely at texts available and found them limited when attempting to find a match with Xiao Yan's experience with using English. Jessica was conscious of carefully considering the supports and challenge of the text offered, looking for possible unfamiliar experiences and difficult language structure. She felt that Xiao Yan would benefit from strengthening her experiences with oral and written language before attempting the more controlled texts in guided reading.

Reading band 4

Chooses to read for interest or to gain specific information. May choose known books from library. Identifies different genres aurally. Reads independently most of the time and with fair understanding. Can read a text for meaning when not all vocabulary is known and be able to identify main points. Interprets maps, graphics and diagrams. Makes a simple critical response to a text or story. Has developed skills in sight organization of discourse, although teacher explanations may be needed for reinforcement. Can read aloud fluently. Pronunciation tends to be correct.

During independent writing time, it was observed that she was beginning to experiment with familiar letters as symbols with some evidence of sound–symbol association. Jessica prompted Xiao Yan to tell her about her pictures and her writing, then scribed her message for her, demonstrating how oral language can be written down. These scribed sentences where made into books which Xiao Yan enjoyed reading to buddies. They also provided a forum for developing concepts about print and most importantly allowed her to recognize the importance of making meaning when reading.

Writing band 4

Writes in sentences a short story that has a beginning, a middle and an end. Redrafts a piece of writing after a writing conference. Makes corrections to own writing after rereading. Shows an awareness of purpose and audience in choice of vocabulary and style. Uses consistent verb tense. Uses writing to argue, convince or justify. Can write simple descriptions, recounts and procedural text. Works independently when writing but asks for help if needed. Uses a variety of strategies to check spelling. Uses commas to separate items in a list. Can use simple past and future tenses where appropriate. Can use articles correctly. May show confusion over conjunctions and tenses. Uses appropriate verb forms in response to a question that models the form.

5. Maryanne's language and literacy profile

Maryanne is presently in fifth grade in Brooklyn, NY. Her story is similar to that of many newcomers who are difficult to place because general assumptions, rather than precise judgments, are made about their progress in using English.

Maryanne arrived in the United States with her mother late in 1998 when she was seven, having spent two years at school in Haiti. Her father had immigrated to the United States two years before that. Her family speaks Haitian Creole at home. In her former school English was the language of instruction and so a decision, based on her schooling history, was made to admit her to second grade.

Maryanne was placed in a mainstream classroom, but, after the teacher noticed that she was not participating in the planned activities, a decision was made to have her assessed to see if she could receive services offered to ESL students. She was assessed, and a decision was made to include her in the school's ESL program, which meant that she was transferred to a self-contained ESL classroom where she worked with a group of students who spoke the same language as she does.

However, Maryanne's behavior changed. She started to act out and became difficult to manage. She would not remain in her seat, and during focus sessions such as Shared Reading and Modeled Writing, became quite disruptive. Her teachers became concerned about the affect on this on others. Her parents were asked to attend a meeting where the decision was made to return Maryanne to her original second-grade class. This meant that she would not receive specialized ESL support either in the class, or be withdrawn for those services.

Maryanne's teacher last year in fourth grade was Heather. Heather noticed that Maryanne really enjoyed writing, and helped her during modeled writing and guided writing sessions get her thoughts onto paper. This was done with a mix of English and Haitian. The resulting writing is a kind of 'pidgin' which contains both English and Creole. The further the year went, the more comfortable Maryanne became as a writer, and used more English and less Creole.

Maryanne remains quite a difficult student at other times, but during writing workshop, and shared reading, enjoys participating, and is obviously using these opportunities to refine her use of English. At lunch she meets with a group of friends, all English speakers, and converses with them.

Band 6 of the ESL scales has indicators that match what Maryanne can do. If Heather had had them available to use she would be able to listen for more specific behaviors about what Maryanne could do and understand her growth more fully.

Maryann's reading is at the early fluency level, and her progress, as a reader does not match that of her development as a writer. Heather observes her progress by using running records, and has noticed that Maryanne has started to monitor her reading, and make self-corrections, rather than just focusing on decoding. It seems as though Maryanne is using her increasing knowledge of English, and her background knowledge to check to see whether her errors when reading make sense and sound right.

Now we can observe Maryann after two months in fifth grade. If we focus on Maryanne's speaking and listening, we see that she enjoys going to art once a week with her class. This is a double period and involves a class meeting, group interaction, individual project work and oral sharing of work and ideas at the end of the period. She works with the whole class during the initial meetings but rarely contributes unless directly called on, She speaks very softly, and relies of the teacher to prompt and question her. However, in a small group situation she becomes animated and often gets involved in a lively discussion, if there are no adults close by. If a teacher leads the group she becomes passive again. She follows the oral instructions of the teacher quite well and when working at her art objects on her own often becomes involved in casual discussions with children working nearby.

Using the ESL Speaking and Listening Scales, the teacher would be able plan for Maryann's growth. For example, she has observed the highlighted behaviors as part of what Maryann can do. Heather could then work out how to scaffold further growth through just a glance at the unhighlighted indicators. In fact she doesn't know if Maryanne can, for example, use pronouns effectively. This use is a strong indicator of English-speaking efficiency.

In shared reading Maryanne is usually seated at the front of the group, near the big book or chart. This is a move made by the teacher to provide Maryanne with the support of those around her. She follows the teacher's voice and pointer with her eyes, and often joins in on a re-reading. However, she rarely reads aloud on the first reading. In guided reading, Maryanne listens closely to the discussion during the book introduction, and follows prompts by the teacher. She is able to make good predictions and can justify them by referring to text and illustrations when asked. She is able to retell, and used some of the language of the book, but finds responding orally a little difficult. She loves to illustrate passages from a book read in guided reading, and will discuss these in a conference with Heather, her teacher.

Using information from the previous year and this year Heather could use the reading scales to find pointers of what she could look for in Maryanne's reading and also to see what she could learn next.

Speaking and listening band 6

Talks individually about own experience to adults. Can describe a sequence of events, join ideas using 'and' or 'then'. Describes objects in detail. Uses known vocabulary and knowledge of discourse to promote a conversation. Contributes information in a small group work situation. Expresses own ideas effectively but not necessarily using correct structures to convey meaning. Begins to use pronouns appropriately. Communicates shades of meaning in a limited way. Constructs simple sentences with words in conventional order. Recounts news, events in the immediate past or past experiences. Offers news or information in a whole-class situation. Can retell parts of stories and repeat rhymes, particularly repetitive ones. Can relay simple messages. Uses common time markers. May speak to mother tongue peers in both first language and English. Actively participates in small group and classroom discussions. Can give opinions with some explanations, express likes and dislikes and answer questions in class. Makes suggestions when problem solving in small group.

Reading band 2

Relies heavily on key words in a text and on extensive teacher support for understanding. Can recognize some signs, labels, letters and numerals. Identifies and names some letters out of context. Sequences a known story using pictures. Demonstrates a sight vocabulary in English, comprised of words that have been covered in class activities. Reads back own writing, or sentences scribed by teacher from own dictation. Can read a well-known text with support. Can track under words while reading. Knows and uses some of the terminology of reading. Understands the function of some punctuation. Demonstrates an understanding of short familiar passages with a simple, repetitive language pattern. Chooses to look at books independently. Chooses books on topics of interest to take home. Can find words in dictionary or from class word lists. Recognizes the difference between English and other languages that use the same script.

class TPa
October 4, 2001
family

my mom I love mom because when I said
buy something and she go buy for
me and when I said let's go
outside and my brother when
I am very very Sad and He come To Play
with me and my father every Time
He telm me what do you To eat Thats

class tPa
October 15, 2001

I remember when I was Haiti
with my grand-mother every day He for me
not be late at school and one day gave
Her envlope and I was go to florida with
my father when I am came my grand-mother
was died and everytime i think my
grand-mother i am crying! the end

6. Jennifer's language and literacy profile

Jennifer spent her pre-school years in China with her grandmother while her parents lived and worked in Australia. When she returned to Australia, because of her age she was placed in first grade. She had no English and had not attended school in China. In the second half of the year a decision was made to place her on the reading recovery program. It was interesting to see how learning to read and learning English went hand-in-hand. She is currently in third grade and is participating in an ESL group for three sessions a week. She says little during whole class times but in a small group she is very comfortable about contributing her ideas. Joanne, her teacher, knows about Jennifer's growth as a language and literacy learner because she is continually observing her in the classroom. The only test she uses are running records that confirm what Jennifer is doing well and what she could be helped to learn.

Speaking and listening in science

ESL group participation involves oral language development based on hands-on science experiences with a small group. This small group work is providing Jennifer with many opportunities to practice her English in both formal and informal situations. There are many indications that her command of English is growing:

Jennifer is able to understand the teacher's questions and respond appropriately and follow oral instructions and directions. She is beginning to become involved in more casual exchanges with her peers and the teacher in this group.

She has prepared and delivered short reports and retold information accurately on topics studied in class. Her oral language shows she has grasped many of the grammatical structures of English.

She generally speaks in sentences, uses pronouns correctly and uses some common contractions with confidence.

She needs assistance with some verb endings and plurals.

Guided reading and shared reading

Jennifer works daily in a guided reading group where she is given time to browse through new texts and discuss the storyline and pictures with the teacher and other group members. There are many indicators that the teacher uses to describe her growth as a reader:

Jennifer is able to use titles, personal experience and knowledge of the topic to predict content and text types. Texts that have supportive illustrations and diagrams and a predictable structure assist her to gain meaning.

She reads confidently, has an excellent memory for words and uses a large repertoire of common sight vocabulary.

She is generally able to maintain the meaning of the text and sometimes asks if there is a word or phrase she does not understand.

She is able to work out unknown words using a range of strategies and will sometimes self-correct at the word level if the visual cues don't match.

Her fluency has shown improvement over the last few months and she takes note of punctuation when reading aloud.

She is able to discuss the story and answer questions.

She is able to read and retell ideas and events from well-known texts and can read and respond to short texts through spoken, written and graphic representations.

The teacher can plan to scaffold Jennifer's learning by helping her work on re-reading sentences when the meaning is lost and on checking word endings such as 'ed' and 's' that she still often omits from words.

As Jennifer seems to have most trouble with nouns, the teacher must think about how help her increase her vocabulary.

Guided and shared writing

Jennifer participates weekly in a guided writing group within the classroom in order to give her the support she needs to compose her work. This has helped her to think things through and organize her thoughts before she begins. Writing with a partner has proved a useful way of providing ongoing support. The teacher has made detailed observations about Jennifer's writing:

Jennifer expresses her ideas and thoughts clearly in writing and is able to write texts that are logically connected when recounting her own experiences.

She can write letters, simple descriptions of things, events, places and simple procedures.

She has begun to use stories she has heard and includes literary phrases she recalls from the story.

Jennifer has an excellent memory for words and has an extensive list of words she writes quickly and fluently. She is able to use known words to assist her to get to unknown ones.

She uses direct speech, pronouns, time sequences and punctuation correctly.

The teacher can scaffold learning by encouraging Jennifer to work on proof reading her work as she writes to make sure it is in the correct tense and that her ideas make sense and flow in a logical order.

She also needs more work on plurals.

The teacher has noticed that she finds it more difficult to express herself clearly when writing imaginative texts and plans to read more of this genre to the class so they can discuss them in literature circles.

The observations made by Joanne are typical of a teacher talking about their students. The ESL profiles have been developed from teachers' knowledge about language and literacy growth for ESL students. They provide a common language and describe what students at various levels of experience would generally be doing. Joanne can easily find Jennifer's place on the ESL profiles by highlighting the indicators that have been observed. It is apparent that Jennifer has shown excellent progress to band 3 and is now even showing some band 4 indicators.

Once there live a poor shoemaker who had a wife. They live right under a work shop which he own himself. One day he went outside to buy some leather for a pair of shoe. One day he went outside for a walk. Then he want to finish the shoe the nex day. But when the shoemaker came back they were already done for him. He shoute "Darling Darling come here quickly" "What is the matter" cried the wife.

Teacher: This book is called Kerry. What do you think it will be about?

Jennifer: It's about a boy who have a dog.

Teacher: Who do you think Kerry is?

Jennifer: Kerry must be the dog because it's a girl's name. I have Kerry in my grade and she's a girl.

Teacher: If you had a dog what would you call it?

Jennifer: Isabella.

Teacher: Why Isabella? Do you know someone named Isabella?

Jennifer: I just make it up. I like that name. My mum, she like that name too.

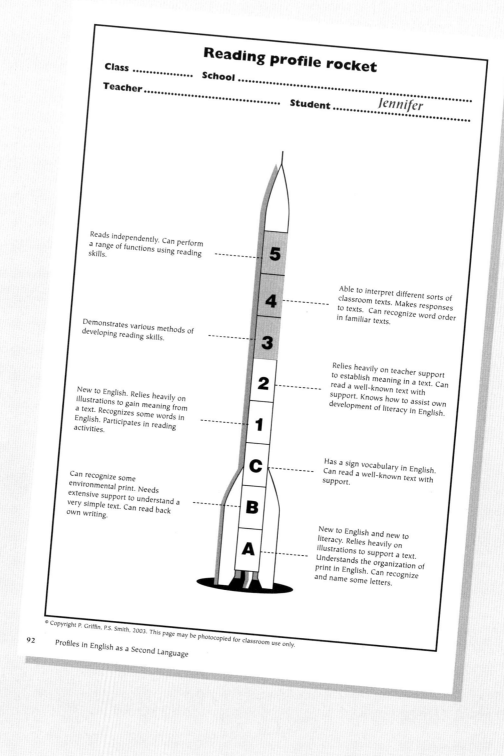

Reading profile rocket

Class .... School ....

Teacher ....

Student .... *Jennifer*

5 Reads independently. Can perform a range of functions using reading skills.

4 Able to interpret different sorts of classroom texts. Makes responses to texts. Can recognize word order in familiar texts.

3 Demonstrates various methods of developing reading skills.

2 Relies heavily on teacher support to establish meaning in a text. Can read a well-known text with support. Knows how to assist own development of literacy in English.

1 New to English. Relies heavily on illustrations to gain meaning from a text. Recognizes some words in English. Participates in reading activities.

C Has a sign vocabulary in English. Can read a well-known text with support.

B Can recognize some environmental print. Needs extensive support to understand a very simple text. Can read back own writing.

A New to English and new to literacy. Relies heavily on illustrations to support a text. Understands the organization of print in English. Can recognize and name some letters.

92   Profiles in English as a Second Language

Figure 2.5 Example rocket report on reading

Chapter 3

Speaking and listening profile records

SPEAKING and LISTENING band  1

Nutshell statement

Settling into situations where English is the dominant language. Discovering that communication with peers and teachers needs to be conducted in English.
Discovering importance of non-verbal communication.

Contexts for observation

- Activities that capture attention and encourage students in their attempts to understand.
- Observing, talking to and listening to students during individual or group activities and in free activity sessions.
- Group story-reading using short, simple, repetitive picture story books.
- Simple rhymes, songs, chants.

What students may do

Initiate conversations with mother tongue peers
Seek explanation of classroom instructions or routines

Use first language with teacher or mother tongue peers

Interpret and respond appropriately to some non-verbal cues

Repeat simple words or phrases appropriately in context
T: What's this? S: What's this?

Repeat the words of other English speakers without comprehension, e.g. with a group of other students or following the lead of another student
Pay attention; laugh; clap

Repeat modeled utterances of very short phrases with understanding

*Left margin tabs: Writing, Reading, **Speaking and listening**; number tabs 9 8 7 6 5 4 3 2 **1***

Name .... Arrival date.....................

Class .... Age .... Languages spoken at home ....

Speaking and listening band I Initiates conversations with mother tongue peers. Interprets and responds appropriately to some non-verbal cues. Repeats the words of other speakers without comprehension. Repeats simple words or phrases appropriately in context. May use first language with teacher or mother tongue peers. Repeats modeled utterances of very short phrases with understanding, usually with a group of other learners.	Comment
Speaking and listening band 2 Initiates conversations with mother tongue peers. Interprets and responds appropriately to some non-verbal cues. Repeats the words of other speakers without comprehension. Repeats simple words or phrases appropriately in context. May use first language with teacher or mother tongue peers. Repeats modeled utterances of very short phrases with understanding, usually with a group of other learners.	Comment

Suggested new indicators

Writing   Reading   **Speaking and listening**

9 8 7 6 5 4 3 2 1

SPEAKING and LISTENING band 2

Communicates simply using a mixture of words, phrases and non-verbal language.
Some communication skills transferred from first language to English.
Takes part in everyday activities and routines. Models behavior on peers.

Contexts for observation

- Observation of response to everyday classroom situations, e.g. demonstration of an activity, getting organized for an art session.
- Simple oral cloze on well-known stories, rhymes, songs
- Appropriate use of some formulae, e.g. greetings, requests
- Use of key words in correct context, e.g. cut, miss?

What students may do

Respond to greetings or to questions in context using facial expressions or gestures

Show understanding of instructions by responding appropriately
T: Color the pictures and then cut them out

Join in well-rehearsed and well-known songs, rhymes, etc., following the model of peers

Indicate objects or characters in pictures that accompany a known story
Big books where the context is known

Observe agreed rules for classroom discourse
Raise hand in large group situations; take turns

Listen for and respond to key words in a sentence
T: Now what did I do with my pencil?
S: Pencil, Miss?
T: It's lunchtime now!
S: Lunch, Miss?

Use a memorized expression to gain a specific response
'May I go to the toilet, please?'

Use intonation to differentiate question and statement
T: What's this?
S: Book
S: Book, Miss? (when looking for last book).

Recognize, use and respond to some informal greetings, introductions and farewells
'Good morning.'; 'How are you?'; 'Fine, thank you.'

Answer questions with a single word or phrase
Clear context and well-known vocabulary, one-to-one or class.
T: What do plants need?
S: Water.
T: Are the three bears angry?
S: Yes angry!

Name .... Arrival date ....

Class .... Age .... Languages spoken at home ....

	Comment
Speaking and listening band 1 Initiates conversations with mother tongue peers. Interprets and responds appropriately to some non-verbal cues. Repeats the words of other speakers without comprehension. Repeats simple words or phrases appropriately in context. May use first language with teacher or mother tongue peers. Repeats modeled utterances of very short phrases with understanding, usually with a group of other learners.	
Speaking and listening band 2 Responds to greetings or to questions in context using facial expressions or gestures. Shows understanding of basic instructions by responding appropriately. Can join in well-rehearsed and well-known songs, rhymes, etc. following the model of peers. May use a memorized expression to gain a specific response or use key words from a formulaic expression. Can answer questions in small groups with a simple word or phrase where the context is clear and the vocabulary well known. Listens for and responds to key words in a sentence. Uses basic intonation to differentiate question and statement. Observes agreed rules for classroom discourse. Recognizes, uses and responds to some informal greetings, introductions and farewells. Speaks at a volume appropriate to the situation.	**Comment**
Speaking and listening band 3 Can use own simple constructions. May use simple adjectives to describe or add emphasis. Responds to questions from peers or teachers with a single word or phrase. Makes simple requests to satisfy immediate needs, using non-verbal language as well as simple expressions. May initiate communication in a small group. Borrows key words from previous speaker. Shows confidence in familiar class and school routines by responding appropriately to instructions and asking for some clarification. May use structures and copy stress and intonation patterns from familiar repetitive stories, songs and rhymes. Uses some appropriate terminology when requesting. Demonstrates active listening. Enhances speaking by using a variety of non-verbal conventions. Understands that talk can affect other people.	**Comment**

Suggested new indicators

Writing   Reading   **Speaking and listening**

9 8 7 6 5 4 3 2 1

SPEAKING and LISTENING band 3

Nutshell statement

Communicates simply in English.
Takes part in everyday activities and routines.
Experiments with the structure of English.
Increases knowledge of English by borrowing from other speakers and familiar sources.

Contexts for observation

- Simple questioning in context.
- General observation and simple questioning, e.g. modification, repetition and modeling of vocabulary and structure.

What students may do

Use own simple constructions
'Him hit me.' 'Yesterday go the beach.'; 'Where toilet?'; 'What this?'

Use simple adjectives to describe or add emphasis
Big truck; Melbourne cold

Respond to questions from peers or teachers with single word or phrase
'Yes.'; 'No.'; 'I don't know.'

Recognize rhyming words
In a listening game

Borrow key words from previous speaker
T: Don't be silly, Tim.
S: Tim silly, Miss.

Show confidence by responding appropriately to instructions and ask for clarification
In familiar class and school routines, e.g. 'No good.'; 'Miss, paper.'; 'Me go.'; 'This one?'

Use structures from familiar repetitive stories, songs and rhymes
'I want some, give me some.' (The Hungry Giant)

Copy stress and intonation patterns from stories, songs and rhymes
Use some appropriate polite terminology when requesting, etc.
'Please.'; 'Thank you.'; 'No thank you.'

Demonstrate active listening and enhance speaking by using a variety of non-verbal conventions
Gesture, eye contact and facial expression

Understand that talk can affect other people
Words of encouragement making people feel good, and negative comments making people feel unhappy

Name .... Arrival date ....

Class .... Age .... Languages spoken at home ....

Speaking and listening band 2

Responds to greetings or to questions in context using facial expressions or gestures. Shows understanding of basic instructions by responding appropriately. Can join in well-rehearsed and well-known songs, rhymes, etc. following the model of peers. May use a memorized expression to gain a specific response or use key words from a formulaic expression. Can answer questions in small groups with a simple word or phrase where the context is clear and the vocabulary well known. Listens for and responds to key words in a sentence. Uses basic intonation to differentiate question and statement. Observes agreed rules for classroom discourse. Recognizes, uses and responds to some informal greetings, introductions and farewells. Speaks at a volume appropriate to the situation.

Comment

Speaking and listening band 3

Can use own simple constructions. May use simple adjectives to describe or add emphasis. Responds to questions from peers or teachers with a single word or phrase. Makes simple requests to satisfy immediate needs, using non-verbal language as well as simple expressions. May initiate communication in a small group. Borrows key words from previous speaker. Shows confidence in familiar class and school routines by responding appropriately to instructions and asking for some clarification. May use structures and copy stress and intonation patterns from familiar repetitive stories, songs and rhymes. Uses some appropriate terminology when requesting. Demonstrates active listening. Enhances speaking by using a variety of non-verbal conventions. Understands that talk can affect other people.

Comment

Speaking and listening band 4

Can respond to 'Wh' questions in context or to short simple questions. Begins to use 'Wh' question forms, not necessarily accurately. May communicate complex situations using English and non-verbal means. Uses simple English in order to communicate in social situations. Asks what a word means. Uses learned formulaic phrases to meet needs but may not be able to use them correctly in new situations. Has a repertoire of common classroom phrases. Uses the language of play at a basic level. Tries to initiate activities with peers using simple English. Uses some social conventions appropriately. Can express humor and describe feelings.

Comment

Suggested new indicators

Writing   Reading   **Speaking and listening**   9 8 7 6 5 4 **3** 2 1

Uses English to communicate simple messages.
Able to indicate time and tense.
Can express simple opinions and ideas.

Contexts for observation

- Games or group activities.
- Verbal retelling of a story, taking turns in a group to complete a story or provide a different ending for a story.
- Modeling of structure and vocabulary.
- Show-and-tell or daily news session, reporting on weekend activities, etc.
- Group problem-solving activities.

What students may do

Respond to 'Wh' questions in context or to short simple questions
Use simple 'Wh' question forms, e.g. 'Where you live?'

Communicate complex situations using English and non-verbal means
Resolving conflict: 'I go play ball, him take ball.'

Use simple English in order to communicate in social situations
'You brother name?'; 'Brother name Khanh.'

As what a word means
'What you mean'?; 'What mean festival?'

Use learned formulaic phrases to meet needs but may not be able to use them correctly in new situations
'May I go to the canteen, please?'; 'Go library, Miss?'

Have a repertoire of common classroom phrases
'Hang on.'; 'Shut up.';. 'Give me hand.'; 'Be quiet, please.'; 'Give me pen.'; 'Can I have a pen, please.'

Use the language of play at a basic level
'I won.'; 'Your turn.'

Try to initiate activities with peers using simple English
'We play.'; 'We go.'

Use some social conventions appropriately
Greetings

Express humor and describe feelings
'Lun happy, Miss. New girlfriend.'

Name .... Arrival date......................

Class .... Age .... Languages spoken at home ....

Speaking and listening band 3	Comment
Can use own simple constructions. May use simple adjectives to describe or add emphasis. Responds to questions from peers or teachers with a single word or phrase. Makes simple requests to satisfy immediate needs, using non-verbal language as well as simple expressions. May initiate communication in a small group. Borrows key words from previous speaker. Shows confidence in familiar class and school routines by responding appropriately to instructions and asking for some clarification. May use structures and copy stress and intonation patterns from familiar repetitive stories, songs and rhymes. Uses some appropriate terminology when requesting. Demonstrates active listening. Enhances speaking by using a variety of non-verbal conventions. Understands that talk can affect other people.	
Speaking and listening band 4	Comment
Can respond to 'Wh' questions in context or to short simple questions. Begins to use 'Wh' question forms, not necessarily accurately. May communicate complex situations using English and non-verbal means. Uses simple English in order to communicate in social situations. Asks what a word means. Uses learned formulaic phrases to meet needs but may not be able to use them correctly in new situations. Has a repertoire of common classroom phrases. Uses the language of play at a basic level. Tries to initiate activities with peers using simple English. Uses some social conventions appropriately. Can express humor and describe feelings.	
Speaking and listening band 5	Comment
Uses most simple 'Wh' questions appropriately. Can transfer known structures to a new situation. Learns English from sources other than the classroom. May ask for names of colors, numbers and interest words. Collects new words from new experiences. Uses key words related to a topic. Can recite a known rhyme, song or chant in an appropriate situation. Makes spontaneous comments in context. Expresses a simple opinion about class texts or events. Relates a simple story or recounts a series of events. May over-generalize a grammatical rule.	

Suggested new indicators

Writing   Reading   **Speaking and listening**

9 8 7 6 5 4 3 2 1

SPEAKING and LISTENING band

Nutshell statement

Expands vocabulary through many different sources. Gaining a stronger structural control of English through experimentation.

Contexts for observation

- Cooperative writing in small groups about excursions.
- Straightforward, cooperative cloze activities.
- Acting out of dialogues requiring creative use of structures already learned.

What students may do

Use most simple 'Wh' questions appropriately
Who; what; where; why; when

Transfer known structures to a new situation
'May I go to play/lunch/the toilet?'

Learn English from sources other than the classroom
Student sees photo in magazine: 'Madonna, you like?'; 'Madonna, good.' (student/student)

Ask for names of colors, numbers, interest words
Dinosaur; greenhouse

Collect new words from new experiences
Excursions; performances (in an appropriate situation)

Use key words related to a topic
Technical vocabulary in science reports

Recite a known rhyme, song or chant
Make spontaneous comments or express an opinion about class texts or events
'The lions were best.' (zoo excursion)

Relate a simple story or recount a series of events
Over-generalize a grammatical rule
'Mouses'; 'sheeps'; 'I goes.'

Name .... Arrival date ....

Class .... Age .... Languages spoken at home ....

Speaking and listening band 4 Can respond to 'Wh' questions in context or to short simple questions. Begins to use 'Wh' question forms, not necessarily accurately. May communicate complex situations using English and non-verbal means. Uses simple English in order to communicate in social situations. Asks what a word means. Uses learned formulaic phrases to meet needs but may not be able to use them correctly in new situations. Has a repertoire of common classroom phrases. Uses the language of play at a basic level. Tries to initiate activities with peers using simple English. Uses some social conventions appropriately. Can express humor and describe feelings.	Comment
Speaking and listening band 5 Uses most simple 'Wh' questions appropriately. Can transfer known structures to a new situation. Learns English from sources other than the classroom. May ask for names of colors, numbers and interest words. Collects new words from new experiences. Uses key words related to a topic. Can recite a known rhyme, song or chant in an appropriate situation. Makes spontaneous comments in context. Expresses a simple opinion about class texts or events. Relates a simple story or recounts a series of events. May over-generalize a grammatical rule.	Comment
Speaking and listening band 6 Talks individually about own experience to adults. Can describe a sequence of events, join ideas using 'and' or 'then'. Describes objects in detail. Uses known vocabulary and knowledge of discourse to promote a conversation. Contributes information in a small group work situation. Expresses own ideas effectively but not necessarily using correct structures to convey meaning. Begins to use pronouns appropriately. Communicates shades of meaning in a limited way. Constructs simple sentences with words in conventional order. Recounts news, events in the immediate past or past experiences. Offers news or information in a whole-class situation. Can retell parts of stories and repeat rhymes, particularly repetitive ones. Can relay simple messages. Uses common time markers. May speak to mother tongue peers in both first language and English. Actively participates in small group and classroom discussions. Can give opinions with some explanations, express likes and dislikes and answer questions in class. Makes suggestions when problem solving in small group.	Comment

Suggested new indicators

Writing Reading **Speaking and listening** 1 2 3 4 **5** 6 7 8 9

SPEAKING and LISTENING band 6

Nutshell statement

Independently communicates experiences with peers and others in a limited way.
Sentences contain simple connectives, some pronouns, rudimentary structures and simple descriptors.

Contexts for observation

- Small group activities based on information and opinion gaps.
- Activities such as retelling stories and recounting news.
- Peer and cross-age tutoring. Speaking in mother tongue may be appropriate.

What students may do

Talk individually about own experience to adults

Describe a sequence of events, join ideas using 'and', 'then'

Describe objects in detail
Color; size; quantity

Use known vocabulary and knowledge of discourse to promote a conversation

Contribute information in a small group work situation

Express own ideas effectively not necessarily using correct structures

Use pronouns appropriately
I/me; he/she

Communicate shades of meaning in a limited way
'Very, very sad'; 'play in water'; 'swim in water'

Construct simple sentences using conventional order
'The car hit the bus.'

Recount news and/or events in the immediate past or past experiences
Whole-class situation

Retell parts of stories and rhymes, particularly repetitive ones
Fairy tales and legends

Relay simple messages
From the ESL teacher to the class teacher

Use common time markers
This morning; last night; next week

Speak to mother tongue peers in both first language and English

Actively participate in small group and classroom discussions
Give opinions, express likes and dislikes and answer questions in class

Make suggestions when problem solving in a small group

Name .... Arrival date ....

Class .... Age .... Languages spoken at home ....

Speaking and listening band 5 Uses most simple 'Wh' questions appropriately. Can transfer known structures to a new situation. Learns English from sources other than the classroom. May ask for names of colors, numbers and interest words. Collects new words from new experiences. Uses key words related to a topic. Can recite a known rhyme, song or chant in an appropriate situation. Makes spontaneous comments in context. Expresses a simple opinion about class texts or events. Relates a simple story or recounts a series of events. May over-generalize a grammatical rule.	Comment
Speaking and listening band 6 Talks individually about own experience to adults. Can describe a sequence of events, join ideas using 'and' or 'then'. Describes objects in detail. Uses known vocabulary and knowledge of discourse to promote a conversation. Contributes information in a small group work situation. Expresses own ideas effectively but not necessarily using correct structures to convey meaning. Begins to use pronouns appropriately. Communicates shades of meaning in a limited way. Constructs simple sentences with words in conventional order. Recounts news, events in the immediate past or past experiences. Offers news or information in a whole-class situation. Can retell parts of stories and repeat rhymes, particularly repetitive ones. Can relay simple messages. Uses common time markers. May speak to mother tongue peers in both first language and English. Actively participates in small group and classroom discussions. Can give opinions with some explanations, express likes and dislikes and answer questions in class. Makes suggestions when problem solving in small group.	Comment
Speaking and listening band 7 Can modify spoken language in a variety of situations. Can use extended speech to communicate additional information. Participates in small group discussions. Uses gestures and fillers to sustain a conversation. Retells a story using mostly words from the story. Substitutes words or phrases appropriately in learned expressions. Uses previously learned grammatical structures. Gives specific directions. Can use 'and/but', 'here/there', 'this/that', 'these/those' appropriately. Chooses to explain things in English to other students. Can request or accept opinions or express a choice of option when problem solving in small group. May volunteer answers to teacher questions directed to the whole class. Can talk about own cultural background. Reads or repeats a sentence accurately using appropriate rhythm and intonation.	Comment
Suggested new indicators	

Writing   Reading   **Speaking and listening**

9 8 7 **6** 5 4 3 2 1

Communicates in English in a variety of situations.
Relies heavily on a core of learned vocabulary and structures.

Contexts for observation

- Collecting information from teachers, parents and other students through surveys and interviews.
- Giving talks on familiar topics.
- Pair work in which students assist each other, e.g. joint construction of a text.
- Peer tutoring.

What students may do

Modify spoken language in a variety of situations
In the playground; in the classroom; in student–student, and student–teacher exchanges

Use extended speech to communicate additional information
'What's Vietnamese food like?'; 'Like Chinese only different.'

Participate in small group discussions

Use gestures and fillers to sustain a conversation
'mmm'

Retell a story using mostly words from the story

Substitute words or phrases appropriately
In learned expressions

Use previously learned grammatical structures

Give specific directions
'across the road'; 'next to the post office'; 'beside the river'

Use 'and', 'but', 'here/there', 'this/that', 'these/those', appropriately

Choose to explain things to other students in English
Key stages of a science experiment

Request or accept opinions or express a choice of option when problem solving in a small group

Volunteer answers to teacher questions directed to the whole class

Talk about own cultural background
About a custom, food, costume, etc.

Read or repeat a sentence accurately using appropriate rhythm and intonation

Speaking and listening   *Reading   Writing*

9 8 7 6 5 4 3 2 1

Name .... Arrival date......................

Class .... Age .... Languages spoken at home ....

	Comment
Speaking and listening band 6 Talks individually about own experience to adults. Can describe a sequence of events, join ideas using 'and' or 'then'. Describes objects in detail. Uses known vocabulary and knowledge of discourse to promote a conversation. Contributes information in a small group work situation. Expresses own ideas effectively but not necessarily using correct structures to convey meaning. Begins to use pronouns appropriately. Communicates shades of meaning in a limited way. Constructs simple sentences with words in conventional order. Recounts news, events in the immediate past or past experiences. Offers news or information in a whole-class situation. Can retell parts of stories and repeat rhymes, particularly repetitive ones. Can relay simple messages. Uses common time markers. May speak to mother tongue peers in both first language and English. Actively participates in small group and classroom discussions. Can give opinions with some explanations, express likes and dislikes and answer questions in class. Makes suggestions when problem solving in small group.	
Speaking and listening band 7 Can modify spoken language in a variety of situations. Can use extended speech to communicate additional information. Participates in small group discussions. Uses gestures and fillers to sustain a conversation. Retells a story using mostly words from the story. Substitutes words or phrases appropriately in learned expressions. Uses previously learned grammatical structures. Gives specific directions. Can use 'and/but', 'here/there', 'this/that', 'these/those' appropriately. Chooses to explain things in English to other students. Can request or accept opinions or express a choice of option when problem solving in small group. May volunteer answers to teacher questions directed to the whole class. Can talk about own cultural background. Reads or repeats a sentence accurately using appropriate rhythm and intonation.	Comment
Speaking and listening band 8 Uses English in more complex social situations. Asks for repetition, rephrasing or how to say something in English. Can justify and explain. Rephrases questions and answers if they are not understood. Answers questions using 'because'. Responds appropriately to complex questions. Uses new words from class topics or themes in everyday speech. Retells a familiar story using the simple past tense. Expresses own ideas so as to be understood by a mainstream speaker. Is confident enough to give a basic narrative or informative talk. Asks confidently for clarification and definition in conversation. Can self-correct. Engages others in conversation on a range of topics. Expresses an opinion about an issue arising from an abridged or modified text. May elect to work with English-speaking peers rather than own language peers. May correct peers. Experiments with more advanced verb forms. Uses tenses to order events in time. Can recount news or events in the immediate past or past events without assistance. Uses articles with reasonable accuracy. Can join ideas.	Comment

Suggested new indicators

Writing | Reading | **Speaking and listening** | 9 8 7 **7** 6 5 4 3 2 1

SPEAKING and LISTENING band 8

Nutshell statement

English shows increasing structural and functional control. Sufficient confidence in English to self-correct, correct other ESL speakers and ask questions about language.

Contexts for observation

- Students interviewing each other.
- Practicing language for social functions.
- Discussion and sharing of opinions about issues arising from text studies and the media.
- Talks assisted by visuals outside immediate personal experiences.

What students may do

Use English in more complex social situations
To introduce; thank; request

Ask for repetition, rephrasing or ask how to say something in English

Justify and explain

Rephrase questions and answers if they are not understood
In a pair task to find out about other student
Answer questions using 'because'

Respond appropriately to complex questions
What are you going to do when you go to Sydney?
Use new words from class topics or themes in everyday speech
Retell a familiar story using the simple past tense
Express own ideas so as to be understood by a mainstream speaker

Give a basic narrative or informative talk
Class excursion; science experiment; research project

Use intonation and rhythm appropriately to support meaning
To express anger, sarcasm and pleasure

Ask confidently for clarification and definition in conversation

Self-correct, engage others in conversation and make themselves understood
In a variety of contexts on a range of topics

Express an opinion about a issue arising from an abridged or modified text

Elect to work with English-speaking peers rather than own language peers

Correct peers

Experiment with more advanced verbs
Conditionals; perfect tenses

Recount news or events in the immediate past without assistance

Appropriately use definite and indefinite articles
A bread roll; some bread

Join ideas
Using 'but' and 'so'

Name .... Arrival date.......................

Class .... Age .... Languages spoken at home ....

	Comment
Speaking and listening band 7 Can modify spoken language in a variety of situations. Can use extended speech to communicate additional information. Participates in small group discussions. Uses gestures and fillers to sustain a conversation. Retells a story using mostly words from the story. Substitutes words or phrases appropriately in learned expressions. Uses previously learned grammatical structures. Gives specific directions. Can use 'and/but', 'here/there', 'this/that', 'these/those' appropriately. Chooses to explain things in English to other students. Can request or accept opinions or express a choice of option when problem solving in small group. May volunteer answers to teacher questions directed to the whole class. Can talk about own cultural background. Reads or repeats a sentence accurately using appropriate rhythm and intonation.	
Speaking and listening band 8 Uses English in more complex social situations. Asks for repetition, rephrasing or how to say something in English. Can justify and explain. Rephrases questions and answers if they are not understood. Answers questions using 'because'. Responds appropriately to complex questions. Uses new words from class topics or themes in everyday speech. Retells a familiar story using the simple past tense. Expresses own ideas so as to be understood by a mainstream speaker. Is confident enough to give a basic narrative or informative talk. Asks confidently for clarification and definition in conversation. Can self-correct. Engages others in conversation on a range of topics. Expresses an opinion about an issue arising from an abridged or modified text. May elect to work with English-speaking peers rather than own language peers. May correct peers. Experiments with more advanced verb forms. Uses tenses to order events in time. Can recount news or events in the immediate past or past events without assistance. Uses articles with reasonable accuracy. Can join ideas.	
Speaking and listening band 9 Speaks fluently. Initiates conversation with other English-speaking people. Seeks information from an unknown person using questions prepared in advance. Initiates and responds to appropriate communication in different registers with people in authority or in subordinate positions. Can initiate complaint to teacher explaining the situation and negotiating a solution. Uses common tag questions naturally in conversation. Is starting to use complex sentences, not necessarily correctly. Can retell an unfamiliar story using own words. Can give a basic talk on how to do a task. Can direct other students by defining a task in a small group discussion.	

Suggested new indicators

Writing   Reading   **Speaking and listening**

1 2 3 4 5 6 7 8 9

Nutshell statement

Speaks fluently. Uses an increasing variety of structures and subject-specific vocabulary. Can initiate and respond to communication in different registers.

Contexts for observation

- Role-play activities.
- Discussing reasons for true/false statements.
- Conferencing with the teacher and/or other students over a piece of writing, e.g. pre-writing conference in pairs.

What students may do

Speak fluently
Consistently use appropriate intonation, rhythm and stress

Initiate conversation with other English-speaking people
Mainstream teachers or other students on a train or on an excursion

Seek information from an unknown person using questions prepared in advance

Initiate communication in different registers with people in authority or in subordinate positions

Initiate a complaint to teacher explaining the situation and negotiating a solution

Use common tag questions naturally in conversation
'He went last night, didn't he?'

Use subject specific vocabulary appropriately

Use complex sentences
I want to be a farmer when I leave school

Retell an unfamiliar story using own words

Give a basic talk on how to do a task

Direct other students by defining a task in a small group discussions

Name .... Arrival date ....

Class .... Age .... Languages spoken at home ....

Speaking and listening band 8	Comment
Uses English in more complex social situations. Asks for repetition, rephrasing or how to say something in English. Can justify and explain. Rephrases questions and answers if they are not understood. Answers questions using 'because'. Responds appropriately to complex questions. Uses new words from class topics or themes in everyday speech. Retells a familiar story using the simple past tense. Expresses own ideas so as to be understood by a mainstream speaker. Is confident enough to give a basic narrative or informative talk. Asks confidently for clarification and definition in conversation. Can self-correct. Engages others in conversation on a range of topics. Expresses an opinion about an issue arising from an abridged or modified text. May elect to work with English-speaking peers rather than own language peers. May correct peers. Experiments with more advanced verb forms. Uses tenses to order events in time. Can recount news or events in the immediate past or past events without assistance. Uses articles with reasonable accuracy. Can join ideas.	
Speaking and listening band 9	Comment
Speaks fluently. Initiates conversation with other English-speaking people. Seeks information from an unknown person using questions prepared in advance. Initiates and responds to appropriate communication in different registers with people in authority or in subordinate positions. Can initiate complaint to teacher explaining the situation and negotiating a solution. Uses common tag questions naturally in conversation. Is starting to use complex sentences, not necessarily correctly. Can retell an unfamiliar story using own words. Can give a basic talk on how to do a task. Can direct other students by defining a task in a small group discussion.	

Suggested new indicators

Chapter 4

Reading profile records

PRE-LITERATE READING band A

Nutshell statement

New to English and new to literacy.
Relies heavily on illustrations to support a text.
Understands the organization of print in English.
Can recognize and name some letters.

(left margin, vertical) Writing · **Reading** · Speaking and listening · A B C 1 2 3 4 5

Contexts for observation

- Shared book experiences.
- Identification games for letters and simple known words, e.g. names of some animals, colors.
- Predicting activities using titles and pictures.

What students may do

Recognize the difference between text and pictures

Recognize own name in a familiar format in upper or lower case

Recognize the initial letters of own name in other contexts

Identify and name some letters out of context

Know how to handle a book
Hold book the right way up and turn the pages from front to back

Know that reading proceeds from left to right and from top to bottom

Join in group reading activities by repeating words or phrases
Shared book experiences

Show enjoyment of well-known story
Shared book experiences

Choose to 'read' books for enjoyment
Choose a book to take home

Name .... Arrival date ....

Class .... Age .... Languages spoken at home ....

Pre-literate reading band A

Knows the difference between text and pictures. Knows that text can be supported by illustrations. Relies heavily on illustrations to gain meaning from a text. Can recognize own name in a familiar context in upper or lower case. Can recognize the initial letters of own name in other contexts. Identifies and names some letters. Knows how to handle a book by holding it right way up and turning the pages from front to back. Knows that reading proceeds from left to right and from the top to the bottom of the page. Can join in with or repeat words or phrases during group or individual reading. Shows enjoyment of a well-known story. Chooses to 'read' books for enjoyment.

Comment

Pre-literate reading band B

Recognizes some isolated words around the room and in known books. Recognizes letters and numerals in texts. Knows there is a difference between first language script and English if the former is non-Roman. Relies on key words for understanding a story read aloud. Relies heavily on extensive teacher support for understanding. Can recognize some signs and labels. Identifies words and spaces in a sentence on request. Can cut up a sentence into words. Can match words. Sequences a known story using pictures. Reads back own writing. Reads sentences scribed by teacher.

Comment

Suggested new indicators

Writing

Reading

Speaking and listening

A B C 1 2 3 4 5

Nutshell statement

Can recognize some environmental print.
Needs extensive support to understand a very simple text.
Can read back own writing.

Contexts for observation

- Tracking story read by teacher (simple, well-known text).
- Activities in small groups, e.g. sequencing pictures, matching familiar texts to pictures.
- Games using signs, symbols, songs.
- Reading with teacher (simple, well-known text).

What students may do

Recognize isolated words
Environmental print around the room

Recognize letters and numerals in texts

Recognize the difference between mother tongue script and English if the former is non-Roman

Rely on key words for understanding a story read aloud

Rely on extensive teacher support for understanding
Teacher using intonation to reinforce drama, comedy, etc.; pointing out the names of the characters and key names of things; stressing the repetitive parts of the story

Recognize some signs and labels
Advertising symbols

Identify words and spaces in a sentence on request

Cut up a sentence into words

Sequence a known story using pictures

Read own writing

Read sentences scribed by teacher

Name .... Arrival date ....

Class .... Age .... Languages spoken at home ....

Pre-literate reading band A

Knows the difference between text and pictures. Knows that text can be supported by illustrations. Relies heavily on illustrations to gain meaning from a text. Can recognize own name in a familiar context in upper or lower case. Can recognize the initial letters of own name in other contexts. Identifies and names some letters. Knows how to handle a book by holding it right way up and turning the pages from front to back. Knows that reading proceeds from left to right and from the top to the bottom of the page. Can join in with or repeat words or phrases during group or individual reading. Shows enjoyment of a well-known story. Chooses to 'read' books for enjoyment.

Comment

Pre-literate reading band B

Recognizes some isolated words around the room and in known books. Recognizes letters and numerals in texts. Knows there is a difference between first language script and English if the former is non-Roman. Relies on key words for understanding a story read aloud. Relies heavily on extensive teacher support for understanding. Can recognize some signs and labels. Identifies words and spaces in a sentence on request. Can cut up a sentence into words. Can match words. Sequences a known story using pictures. Reads back own writing. Reads sentences scribed by teacher.

Comment

Pre-literate reading band C

Recognizes a number of signs and symbols. Demonstrates a sight vocabulary in English comprised of words that have been covered in class activities. Indicates key words in a known story. Can read a well-known text with support. Can track under words when reading. Knows the difference between English and other languages that use the same script. Uses some of the terminology of reading. Understands the function of some punctuation. Demonstrates an understanding of short familiar passages. Can match words to sentences in a known text. Chooses books on topics of interest to take home. Finds words in own dictionary or from class word lists.

Comment

Suggested new indicators

Writing · Reading · Speaking and listening

A B C 1 2 3 4 5

PRE-LITERATE READING band

C

Has a sign vocabulary in English.
Can read a well-known text with support.

Contexts for observation

- Reading in small groups (simple, well-known text).
- Reading with teacher (simple, well-known text).
- Activities in small groups, e.g. sequencing pictures, matching familiar texts to pictures.
- Games using signs, symbols, songs; intonation games.
- Pre-reading quizzes; true/false statements in small groups or pair work.

What students may do

Recognize signs and symbols
Stop sign; walk/don't walk lights

Demonstrate sight vocabulary in English
Words from familiar stories, songs, etc.

Indicate key words read from known story

Read known text with support

Track under words
Known text

Know the difference between English and other languages that use the same script

Use some of the terminology of reading
Title; author; sentence; picture; word

Understands the function of some punctuation
Know that a full stop breaks up text

Demonstrate an understanding of short familiar passages

Match words to sentences
Known text

Choose books on topics of interest to take home

Find words in own dictionary or from class word lists

Reading profile record

Name .... Arrival date ....

Class .... Age .... Languages spoken at home ....

Pre-literate reading band B Recognizes some isolated words around the room and in known books. Recognizes letters and numerals in texts. Knows there is a difference between first language script and English if the former is non-Roman. Relies on key words for understanding a story read aloud. Relies heavily on extensive teacher support for understanding. Can recognize some signs and labels. Identifies words and spaces in a sentence on request. Can cut up a sentence into words. Can match words. Sequences a known story using pictures. Reads back own writing. Reads sentences scribed by teacher.	Comment
Pre-literate reading band C Recognizes a number of signs and symbols. Demonstrates a sight vocabulary in English comprised of words that have been covered in class activities. Indicates key words in a known story. Can read a well-known text with support. Can track under words when reading. Knows the difference between English and other languages that use the same script. Uses some of the terminology of reading. Understands the function of some punctuation. Demonstrates an understanding of short familiar passages. Can match words to sentences in a known text. Chooses books on topics of interest to take home. Finds words in own dictionary or from class word lists.	Comment

Suggested new indicators

Writing

Reading

Speaking and listening

5 4 3 2 1 C B A

READING band

Nutshell statement

New to English.
Relies heavily on illustrations to gain meaning from a text.
Recognizes some words in English.
Participates in reading activities.

Contexts for observation

- Shared book experiences.
- Reading in small groups.
- Predicting activities using titles and pictures.

What students may do

Know the difference between text and pictures

Use illustrations to support reading

Read own name in full in upper and lower case

Recognize the initial letters of own name in other contexts

Read isolated words
Environmental print in the classroom

Identify some letters and numerals
Out of context

Identify words and spaces in a sentence

Recognize a difference between graphophonic basis of first language and English

Know of how to handle a book
Hold book the right way up and turn the pages from front to back

Recognize that reading in English proceeds from left to right, top to bottom

Join in group reading activities by repeating words or phrases
Shared book experiences

Show enjoyment of a well-known story
Shared book experiences

Choose to 'read' books for enjoyment
Choose a book to take home

Name .... Arrival date......................

Class .... Age .... Languages spoken at home ....

Reading band 1

Knows the difference between text and pictures. Understands that text can be supported by illustrations. Relies heavily on illustrations to gain meaning from a text. Reads own name in full in upper or lower case. Recognizes the initial letters of own name in other contexts. Reads some words around the room or in known books. Can identify some letters and numerals. Identifies words and spaces in a sentence. Recognizes that there is a difference between the graphophonic base of first language and English. Knows how to handle a book. Knows that reading in English proceeds from left to right and from the top to the bottom of the page. Joins in with or repeats words or phrases during a group or individual reading. Shows enjoyment of a well-known story. Chooses to read books for enjoyment.

Comment

Reading band 2

Relies heavily on key words in a text and on extensive teacher support for understanding. Can recognize some signs, labels, letters and numerals. Identifies and names some letters out of context. Sequences a known story using pictures. Demonstrates a sight vocabulary in English, comprised of words that have been covered in class activities. Reads back own writing, or sentences scribed by teacher from own dictation. Can read a well-known text with support. Can track under words while reading. Knows and uses some of the terminology of reading. Understands the function of some punctuation. Demonstrates an understanding of short familiar passages with a simple, repetitive language pattern. Chooses to look at books independently. Chooses books on topics of interest to take home. Can find words in dictionary or from class word lists. Recognizes the difference between English and other languages that use the same script.

Comment

Suggested new indicators

Writing

Reading

Speaking and listening

A B C 1 2 3 4 5

READING
band

Nutshell statement

Relies heavily on teacher support to establish meaning in a text.
Can read a well-known text with support.
Knows how to assist own development of literacy in English.

Contexts for observation

- Reading with teacher.
- Using key words to write own texts and comparing these with original texts.
- Activities in small groups, e.g. sequencing pictures, matching familiar texts to pictures.
- Games using signs, symbols, songs.

What students may do

Rely on key words for understanding
Story read aloud; in a text

Recognize letters and numerals

Recognize some signs and labels
Advertising symbols

Identify and name some letters out of context

Identify words from class activities
Words in songs; stories

Sequence a story using pictures
Familiar story

Read back own work
Read own writing

Read sentence scribed by teacher from own dictation

Read well-known text with support

Track under words
Well-known text

Know and use some of the terminology of reading
Author; title; page

Understand the function of some punctuation
Know that a full stop breaks up the text when reading and that a capital letter starts a sentence

Understand short familiar passages with simple, repetitive language
Completing comprehension activities

Choose to look at books independently

Find words in dictionaries and class word lists

Recognize the difference between English and other languages that use the same script

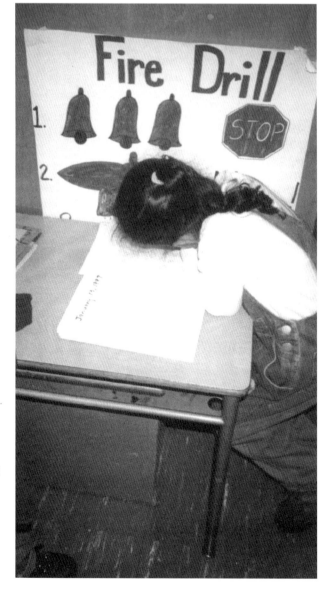

Speaking and listening   Reading   Writing

A B C 1 2 3 4 5

Name .... Arrival date ....

Class .... Age .... Languages spoken at home ....

Reading band 1
Knows the difference between text and pictures. Understands that text can be supported by illustrations. Relies heavily on illustrations to gain meaning from a text. Reads own name in full in upper or lower case. Recognizes the initial letters of own name in other contexts. Reads some words around the room or in known books. Can identify some letters and numerals. Identifies words and spaces in a sentence. Recognizes that there is a difference between the graphophonic base of first language and English. Knows how to handle a book. Knows that reading in English proceeds from left to right and from the top to the bottom of the page. Joins in with or repeats words or phrases during a group or individual reading. Shows enjoyment of a well-known story. Chooses to read books for enjoyment.

Comment

Reading band 2
Relies heavily on key words in a text and on extensive teacher support for understanding. Can recognize some signs, labels, letters and numerals. Identifies and names some letters out of context. Sequences a known story using pictures. Demonstrates a sight vocabulary in English, comprised of words that have been covered in class activities. Reads back own writing, or sentences scribed by teacher from own dictation. Can read a well-known text with support. Can track under words while reading. Knows and uses some of the terminology of reading. Understands the function of some punctuation. Demonstrates an understanding of short familiar passages with a simple, repetitive language pattern. Chooses to look at books independently. Chooses books on topics of interest to take home. Can find words in dictionary or from class word lists. Recognizes the difference between English and other languages that use the same script.

Comment

Reading band 3
Recognizes and uses visual support to help gain meaning from a text. Uses graphophonic cueing to attack new words. Recognizes individual English words. Modifies intonation when reading to differentiate questions, exclamations or dialogue. Recognizes some different genres. Knows when a story is not yet finished. Concentrates during group reading activities. Reads along with others. Reads supportive texts independently. Recalls important details.

Comment

Suggested new indicators

Writing   Reading   Speaking and listening

A   B   C   1   2   3   4   5

Contexts for observation

- Predicting activities.
- Pre-reading quizzes; true/false statements in small groups or pair work.
- Reading with peers.
- Games on intonation.
- Matching simple unfamiliar texts to pictures, diagrams, etc.

What students may do

Use visual support to gain meaning from text
Diagrams, graphs or pictures to predict story, characters, topics

Use graphophonic cueing to attack new words

Recognize individual English words

Modify intonation
To differentiate questions, exclamations or dialogue

Recognize some different genres
Poems; difference between a factual text and a story

Know when a story is not yet finished
Shared book experiences; group reading activities

Concentrate during group reading activities
Shared book experiences

Read along with others
Peers; teachers; a listening post

Read independently
A modified text for ESL students

Recall important details
A modified text for ESL students

Name .... Arrival date ....

Class .... Age .... Languages spoken at home ....

Reading band 2
Relies heavily on key words in a text and on extensive teacher support for understanding. Can recognize some signs, labels, letters and numerals. Identifies and names some letters out of context. Sequences a known story using pictures. Demonstrates a sight vocabulary in English, comprised of words that have been covered in class activities. Reads back own writing, or sentences scribed by teacher from own dictation. Can read a well-known text with support. Can track under words while reading. Knows and uses some of the terminology of reading. Understands the function of some punctuation. Demonstrates an understanding of short familiar passages with a simple, repetitive language pattern. Chooses to look at books independently. Chooses books on topics of interest to take home. Can find words in dictionary or from class word lists. Recognizes the difference between English and other languages that use the same script.

Comment

Reading band 3
Recognizes and uses visual support to help gain meaning from a text. Uses graphophonic cueing to attack new words. Recognizes individual English words. Modifies intonation when reading to differentiate questions, exclamations or dialogue. Recognizes some different genres. Knows when a story is not yet finished. Concentrates during group reading activities. Reads along with others. Reads supportive texts independently. Recalls important details.

Comment

Reading band 4
Chooses to read for interest or to gain specific information. May choose known books from library. Identifies different genres aurally. Reads independently most of the time and with fair understanding. Can read a text for meaning when not all vocabulary is known and be able to identify main points. Interprets maps, graphics and diagrams. Makes a simple critical response to a text or story. Has developed skills in sight organization of discourse, although teacher explanations may be needed for reinforcement. Can read aloud fluently. Pronunciation tends to be correct.

Comment

Suggested new indicators

Writing

Reading

Speaking and listening

A B C 1 2 3 4 5

Speaking and listening Reading Writing

A B C 1 2 3 4 5

Nutshell statement

Able to interpret different sorts of classroom texts.
Makes responses to texts.
Can recognize word order in familiar texts.

Contexts for observation

- Cloze exercises.
- Reading and retelling exercises (with teacher guidance).
- Vocabulary development exercises using contextual clues to derive meanings.
- Answering simple context questions about maps, graphics, diagrams and informational texts such as simple tourist brochures.

What students may do

Read for interest or to gain specific information
Borrow books from library, e.g. on dinosaurs

Read for meaning when not all vocabulary is known
ESL text

Identify main points in story or text
ESL text

Identify different genres aurally
Story; poem; factual account

Read independently most of the time and with fair understanding

Interpret maps, graphics and diagrams
Maps, graphics and diagrams in classroom texts

Make a critical response to a text
By commenting on actions of main characters in a text or story

Correctly sequence word order in a known text
Reorder sentences in which words have been jumbled

Can read aloud fairly fluently with correct pronunciation
ESL texts at an appropriate level

Name .... Arrival date.....................

Class .... Age .... Languages spoken at home ....

Reading band 3 Recognizes and uses visual support to help gain meaning from a text. Uses graphophonic cueing to attack new words. Recognizes individual English words. Modifies intonation when reading to differentiate questions, exclamations or dialogue. Recognizes some different genres. Knows when a story is not yet finished. Concentrates during group reading activities. Reads along with others. Reads supportive texts independently. Recalls important details.	**Comment**
Reading band 4 Chooses to read for interest or to gain specific information. May choose known books from library. Identifies different genres aurally. Reads independently most of the time and with fair understanding. Can read a text for meaning when not all vocabulary is known and be able to identify main points. Interprets maps, graphics and diagrams. Makes a simple critical response to a text or story. Has developed skills in sight organization of discourse, although teacher explanations may be needed for reinforcement. Can read aloud fluently. Pronunciation tends to be correct.	**Comment**
Reading band 5 Can comprehend a range of genres at an appropriate level. Reads independently. Understands ESL and mainstream texts at an appropriate level without teacher explanation. Reads for specific information. Can get the gist of a text by skimming and scanning. Can identify main and supporting ideas in texts. Can work out meanings of some unknown words. Comprehends cultural references. Uses supporting evidence from texts to express own opinions. Applies information acquired through reading to other areas.	**Comment**

Suggested new indicators

Writing Reading Speaking and listening

A B C 1 2 3 4 5

Writing

Reading

Speaking and listening

A B C 1 2 3 4 **5**

Contexts for observation

- Individual independent reading leading to a book review.
- Note-taking exercises for main ideas.
- Written or oral comprehension exercises, e.g. reading a description of how to make something or of a process, and writing or describing main points for class.
- Class discussion on selected aspects of text independently read, e.g. discussion of character in a novel with a view to building a character study.

What students may do

Comprehend a range of genres at an appropriate level

Read independently

Understand texts without teacher explanation
ESL and mainstream texts, for main ideas or for detailed information

Get the gist of a text by skimming and scanning
ESL and mainstream texts

Can identify and differentiate between main ideas and supporting ideas
For summarizing, taking notes, discussion purposes

Can work out meanings of some unknown words
Use clues from text to deduce meaning

Can comprehend cultural references due to broadened cultural knowledge
Idioms, metaphors and subtle humor

Respond to a range of texts using supporting evidence from text

Expressing own opinions about plot and character
ESL and mainstream texts

Use information acquired through reading to make inferences, draw conclusions and apply to broader themes
Relate themes from texts to current media issues

Name .... Arrival date.......................

Class .... Age .... Languages spoken at home ....

Reading band 4 Chooses to read for interest or to gain specific information. May choose known books from library. Identifies different genres aurally. Reads independently most of the time and with fair understanding. Can read a text for meaning when not all vocabulary is known and be able to identify main points. Interprets maps, graphics and diagrams. Makes a simple critical response to a text or story. Has developed skills in sight organization of discourse, although teacher explanations may be needed for reinforcement. Can read aloud fluently. Pronunciation tends to be correct.	**Comment**
Reading band 5 Can comprehend a range of genres at an appropriate level. Reads independently. Understands ESL and mainstream texts at an appropriate level without teacher explanation. Reads for specific information. Can get the gist of a text by skimming and scanning. Can identify main and supporting ideas in texts. Can work out meanings of some unknown words. Comprehends cultural references. Uses supporting evidence from texts to express own opinions. Applies information acquired through reading to other areas.	**Comment**

Suggested new indicators

Writing

Reading

Speaking and listening

A B C 1 2 3 4 **5**

Chapter 5

Writing profile records

PRE-LITERATE WRITING band /A

(Nutshell statement)

New to literacy in English, and perhaps in first language.
Relies heavily on pictures and illustrations to communicate.

Writing

Reading

Speaking and listening

A B C 1 2 3 4 5 6

Contexts for observation

- Drawing activities.
- Games using symbols, letters or copied words.
- Labeling activities.

What students may do

Draw pictures that relate to an ongoing activity or tell a simple story
May repeatedly draw same picture, e.g. house, car, tree, flower, self

Know differences between pictures and print
Picture story book

Write an accompanying text using symbols, letters or copied words
Spontaneously when drawing e.g. attach labels to pictures using environmental print

Attribute simple meaning to own writing
Can indicate (in first language or English) what own 'writing' says

Understand that writing proceeds from left to right
Write letters or symbols from left to right

Show awareness that writing moves from top to bottom of page
Start writing in top left-hand corner

Use a preferred hand for writing and drawing

Hold pen or pencil using an appropriate grip
In drawing or copying words

Write own name
Labeling of belongings, paintings, drawings

Copy words, labels, signs from board, books or charts
Environmental print around room

Show an awareness of some basic sound–symbol relationships

Recognize some letters
T: Have you got this letter in your name?
S: Yes

Copy a sentence scribed by teacher from own dictation
This is a picture of my house

Name .... Arrival date.....................

Class .... Age .... Languages spoken at home ....

Pre-literate writing band A

Draws pictures that relate to an ongoing activity or to tell a story. Knows difference between pictures and print. May write an accompanying text using symbols, letters or copied words. Attributes simple meaning to own writing in English or first language. Uses drawings to support text. Understands that English writing proceeds from left to right and from top to bottom of page. Uses a preferred hand for writing and drawing. Holds pen or pencil using an appropriate grip. Can write own name. May copy words, labels, signs from board, books or charts. Is aware of some sound–symbol relationships. Can recognize some letters. Can copy a simple sentence scribed by teacher from own dictation.

Comment

Pre-literate writing band B

Recognizes some words and attempts to reproduce them. Supports own writing by using drawings. Spoken structures and vocabulary reflected in writing. Can form letters appropriately. Leaves spaces between words. Knows difference between upper and lower case letters. Can copy a short passage correctly from the board or a book. Understands some of the terminology of writing. Can finish off short, modeled sentences with some simple personal information. Can draw to support a simple text. Labels own drawings using copied words. Attempts to spell new words. Attempts to write sentences using appropriate spacing between words and ending with a full stop. Asks for words to use in own writing or labeling. Finds some well-known words in charts, books or word banks to use in own writing. Contributes ideas, sentences or words to a class or group story.

Comment

Suggested new indicators

Speaking and listening   Reading   Writing

A   B   C   1   2   3   4   5   6

PRE-LITERATE WRITING band **B**

Nutshell statement

Can recognize some words and attempts to reproduce them.
Supports own writing by using drawings.
Spoken structures reflected in writing.

Contexts for observation

- Class shared writing activities, e.g. finishing off a sentence.
- Labeling activities.
- Games using symbols, letters or copied words.

What students may do

Recognize some words and attempts to reproduce them

Support own writing with drawings

Form letters appropriately and leave spaces between words
When copying writing or when writing own words

Understand the difference between upper and lower case letters

Copy a short passage correctly
From the board or a book, e.g. Today is Monday.

Understand some terminology of writing
Word; letter; sentence; space; full stop

Finish off short, modeled sentences with personal information
My name is … we went to the (zoo)

Draw to support a simple text
When making a shared book

Label own drawings using copied words
Label a drawing 'My house' from a previous drawing labeled by teacher

Attempt to spell new words
Label a drawing 'Hos'

Attempt to write sentences using appropriate spacing in sentences and appropriate punctuation
May finish sentence with a full stop

Ask for words to use when writing or labeling

Find words in charts, books, word banks to use in own writing
Environmental print; classroom resources

Contribute ideas, sentences or words to a class or group shared story about a shared experience
A class story about a trip to the market

Writing

Reading

Speaking and listening

A B C 1 2 3 4 5 6

Name .... Arrival date ....

Class .... Age .... Languages spoken at home ....

Pre-literate writing band A
Draws pictures that relate to an ongoing activity or to tell a story. Knows difference between pictures and print. May write an accompanying text using symbols, letters or copied words. Attributes simple meaning to own writing in English or first language. Uses drawings to support text. Understands that English writing proceeds from left to right and from top to bottom of page. Uses a preferred hand for writing and drawing. Holds pen or pencil using an appropriate grip. Can write own name. May copy words, labels, signs from board, books or charts. Is aware of some sound–symbol relationships. Can recognize some letters. Can copy a simple sentence scribed by teacher from own dictation.

Comment

Pre-literate writing band B
Recognizes some words and attempts to reproduce them. Supports own writing by using drawings. Spoken structures and vocabulary reflected in writing. Can form letters appropriately. Leaves spaces between words. Knows difference between upper and lower case letters. Can copy a short passage correctly from the board or a book. Understands some of the terminology of writing. Can finish off short, modeled sentences with some simple personal information. Can draw to support a simple text. Labels own drawings using copied words. Attempts to spell new words. Attempts to write sentences using appropriate spacing between words and ending with a full stop. Asks for words to use in own writing or labeling. Finds some well-known words in charts, books or word banks to use in own writing. Contributes ideas, sentences or words to a class or group story.

Comment

Pre-literate writing band C
Attempts to write letters with consistent size, shape and spacing and in straight lines. May use letter size and color to create a particular feel in a text. Begins to use some punctuation. Can copy a longer passage correctly from the board or a book. Writes simple assessments or reports about self from modeled examples. May write the same texts repeatedly. Uses a known story form to begin writing. Shows an awareness of story from by writing a beginning, a middle and an end in own stories. Can choose own topic to write about, often starting from own drawings. Can write own short texts. Can write for a 'real' task. Includes some words spelt conventionally. Attempts to write unknown words may result in unconventional spelling.

Comment

Suggested new indicators

Speaking and listening　Reading　Writing

A B C 1 2 3 4 5 6

PRE-LITERATE WRITING band

C

Nutshell statement

Writing shows greater physical control.
Repetition of familiar texts.
Grasp of story form and own short texts.
Some attempts at conventional spelling.

Contexts for observation

- Copying exercises, e.g. short simple passages.
- Writing two or three simple sentences about self or neighbor.
- Class writing of simple text about excursion.
- Writing a simple shopping list, list of animals, postcard, greeting card.
- Simple dictation exercises.

What students may do

Attempt to write letters with consistent size, shape and spacing and in straight lines

Use letter size and color to create a particular feel in a text
Writing a greeting on a birthday card; designing a poster

Use some punctuation
Full stops; capital letters

Copy a longer text correctly from the board or a book
Today is Monday 27 June. After lunch we are going to the art room

Write simple self-assessments or reports from modeled examples
'I'm …'; 'I like …'; 'I'm good at …'; 'My friends are …'

Write the same texts repeatedly
'My name is …'; 'I come from …'; I went shopping and bought …'

Use a known story form to begin writing
Once upon a time; one day

Show an awareness of story form by writing a beginning, a middle and an end
With support through conferencing

Choose topic to write about, often starting from own drawings

Write own short texts

Write for a 'real' task
Making a list; writing a letter; writing a story at home

Include some words in writing spelt conventionally from a known spelling vocabulary or from a word list, and words using attempts at spelling

Name .... Arrival date......................

Class .... Age .... Languages spoken at home ....

Pre-literate writing band B

Recognizes some words and attempts to reproduce them. Supports own writing by using drawings. Spoken structures and vocabulary reflected in writing. Can form letters appropriately. Leaves spaces between words. Knows difference between upper and lower case letters. Can copy a short passage correctly from the board or a book. Understands some of the terminology of writing. Can finish off short, modeled sentences with some simple personal information. Can draw to support a simple text. Labels own drawings using copied words. Attempts to spell new words. Attempts to write sentences using appropriate spacing between words and ending with a full stop. Asks for words to use in own writing or labeling. Finds some well-known words in charts, books or word banks to use in own writing. Contributes ideas, sentences or words to a class or group story.

Comment

Pre-literate writing band C

Attempts to write letters with consistent size, shape and spacing and in straight lines. May use letter size and color to create a particular feel in a text. Begins to use some punctuation. Can copy a longer passage correctly from the board or a book. Writes simple assessments or reports about self from modeled examples. May write the same texts repeatedly. Uses a known story form to begin writing. Shows an awareness of story from by writing a beginning, a middle and an end in own stories. Can choose own topic to write about, often starting from own drawings. Can write own short texts. Can write for a 'real' task. Includes some words spelt conventionally. Attempts to write unknown words may result in unconventional spelling.

Comment

Suggested new indicators

Writing
Reading
Speaking and listening

A B C 1 2 3 4 5 6

WRITING
band

Nutshell statement

New to literacy in English.
May write in first language.
Attempts to write in English.
Supports writing using illustrations.

Contexts for observation

- Drawing activities.
- Games using symbols, letters or copied words.
- Labeling activities.
- Simple dictation exercises.

What students may do

Write initially in first language

Draw pictures that relate to an ongoing activity or to tell a story
When making a shared book, or an individual book, using modeled sentences

Draw to support text

Write own name in full

Complete short sentences with personal information
'I'm …'; 'I like …'; 'I'm good at …'; 'My friends are …'

Copy a sentence scribed by teacher from own dictation
'My name is … I come from …'

Complete simple, repetitive modeled sentences
About topic recently covered

Copy words, labels, signs from the board, books or charts to use in own writing

Copy text correctly from the board or a book

Use appropriate size, spacing and letter formation

Show an awareness of some English sound–symbol relationships

Name .... Arrival date ....

Class .... Age .... Languages spoken at home ....

Writing band 1 May initially write in first language. Draws pictures that relate to an ongoing activity or to tell a story. Draws to support a text. Writes own name in full. Completes short sentences with personal information. Completes simple, repetitive modeled sentences. Can copy a sentence scribed by teacher from own dictation. Copies words, labels, signs from the board, books or charts to use in own writing. Copies text correctly from the board or a book. Uses appropriate size, spacing, and letter formation. Is aware of some English sound–symbol relationships.	Comment
Writing band 2 Writes or completes simple sentences from own experiences. May write familiar texts repeatedly, based on modeled repetitive structures. Matches written structures and vocabulary to spoken structures and vocabulary. May use 'and', 'then', 'next' to link ideas in a sentence. Can use repetition and choose vocabulary to add emphasis. Asks the names of things in English to use in own writing. Finds words in charts, books and word banks to use in writing. Can maintain own word banks and topic lists. Finds words from word lists and simple dictionaries. Understands some of the terminology of writing. May use some punctuation to break up ideas. Knows that sentences start with a capital letter. Attempts to spell some new words using knowledge of English graphophonic conventions. Asks for the spelling of words to use in own writing. Contributes ideas, sentences or words to a class or group story.	Comment

Suggested new indicators

Writing

Reading

Speaking and listening

A B C 1 2 3 4 5 6

WRITING band

Nutshell statement

Can write simple sentences.
Correlation between written and oral structures and vocabulary.
Consciously seeks to increase range of vocabulary and structures
for writing.

Writing

Reading

Speaking and listening

A   B   C   1   2   3   4   5   6

Contexts for observation

- Class shared writing activities, e.g. finishing off a sentence, writing a story.
- Word games using dictionaries or word banks to extend and reinforce vocabulary.
- Sentence-building exercises.
- Writing two or three simple sentences about self or neighbor.
- Class writing of simple text about excursion.
- Writing a simple shopping list, list of animals, postcard, greeting card.
- Writing simple dictation.

What students may do

Write or complete simple sentences from own experiences
Name; address; country of origin; hair color

Write same texts repeatedly, based on modeled repetitive structures
'On the weekend went shopping and bought …'

Match written structures and vocabulary to spoken structures and vocabulary

Use 'and', 'then', 'next' to link ideas in a sentence

Use repetition and choose vocabulary to add emphasis
'Very, very good.'

Ask the names of things in English to use in own writing

Find words in charts, books, word banks to use in own writing

Maintain own simple dictionaries, topic lists, etc. and find words needed from these

Understand some of the terminology of writing
Word; letter; full stop

Attempt to spell some new words using knowledge of English graphophonic conventions
'rokit' for 'rocket'

Use some punctuation to break up ideas

Know that sentences start with a capital letter

Ask for the spelling of words to use in own writing

Contribute ideas, sentences or words to a class or group story

Name .... Arrival date ....

Class .... Age .... Languages spoken at home ....

Writing band 1 May initially write in first language. Draws pictures that relate to an ongoing activity or to tell a story. Draws to support a text. Writes own name in full. Completes short sentences with personal information. Completes simple, repetitive modeled sentences. Can copy a sentence scribed by teacher from own dictation. Copies words, labels, signs from the board, books or charts to use in own writing. Copies text correctly from the board or a book. Uses appropriate size, spacing, and letter formation. Is aware of some English sound–symbol relationships.	Comment
Writing band 2 Writes or completes simple sentences from own experiences. May write familiar texts repeatedly, based on modeled repetitive structures. Matches written structures and vocabulary to spoken structures and vocabulary. May use 'and', 'then', 'next' to link ideas in a sentence. Can use repetition and choose vocabulary to add emphasis. Asks the names of things in English to use in own writing. Finds words in charts, books and word banks to use in writing. Can maintain own word banks and topic lists. Finds words from word lists and simple dictionaries. Understands some of the terminology of writing. May use some punctuation to break up ideas. Knows that sentences start with a capital letter. Attempts to spell some new words using knowledge of English graphophonic conventions. Asks for the spelling of words to use in own writing. Contributes ideas, sentences or words to a class or group story.	Comment
Writing band 3 Uses a known story form to begin writing. May borrow structures from well-known stories to write own stories. Chooses own topic to write about. Can write a few lines on a topic of interest that has been covered in class. Can write short, factual text independently. Writes own simple journal or diary entries independently. Can write several sentences with connected ideas. Refers back using pronouns. Uses connectives such as 'and', 'but', 'because' to link ideas in short texts. Structures used in writing such as word order may reflect some first language features. Uses capital letters appropriately for proper nouns. Uses some more complex punctuation. Supported by class discussion and activities such as modeling, can retell a narrative in writing. Can provide an alternative ending for a story. Shares writing with a partner or a group. Can name all the English letters and knows the sounds they commonly represent. Can present writing appropriately for different audiences or for display using headings, layout and illustrations. May experiment with lettering.	Comment

Suggested new indicators

Writing   Reading   Speaking and listening

A B C 1 2 3 4 5 6

WRITING band 3

Nutshell statement

Can write for different purposes.
Uses a restricted range of structures and vocabulary.

Writing

Reading

Speaking and listening

A B C 1 2 3 4 5 6

Contexts for observation

- Retelling exercises of short simple passages (with guidance and support).
- Using well-known structures in own original work.
- Small group or pair work, conferencing.
- Journal, diary, letter writing exercises.

What students may do

Use a known story form to begin writing
'Once upon time'; 'One day'

Borrow structures from well-known stories to write own stories

Choose own topic to write about

Write a few lines on a topic of interest that has been covered in class

Write short, factual text independently
Making a list; writing a letter; writing a story at home

Write own simple journal or diary entries independently

Write simple sentences, connect ideas and refer back using pronouns
'Yesterday John went to the zoo. He saw lots of animals there.'

Use connectives to link ideas in short texts
And; but; because

Use capital letters appropriately for proper nouns
People's names; countries; cities

Use some more complex punctuation
Question marks; exclamation marks

Retell a narrative in writing, or provide an alternative ending
For a simple story with extensive teacher support

Share own writing with a partner or a group

Present writing appropriately for different audiences or for display

Experiment with lettering

Name .... Arrival date.....................

Class .... Age .... Languages spoken at home ....

Writing band 2

Writes or completes simple sentences from own experiences. May write familiar texts repeatedly, based on modeled repetitive structures. Matches written structures and vocabulary to spoken structures and vocabulary. May use 'and', 'then', 'next' to link ideas in a sentence. Can use repetition and choose vocabulary to add emphasis. Asks the names of things in English to use in own writing. Finds words in charts, books and word banks to use in writing. Can maintain own word banks and topic lists. Finds words from word lists and simple dictionaries. Understands some of the terminology of writing. May use some punctuation to break up ideas. Knows that sentences start with a capital letter. Attempts to spell some new words using knowledge of English graphophonic conventions. Asks for the spelling of words to use in own writing. Contributes ideas, sentences or words to a class or group story.

Comment

Writing band 3

Uses a known story form to begin writing. May borrow structures from well-known stories to write own stories. Chooses own topic to write about. Can write a few lines on a topic of interest that has been covered in class. Can write short, factual text independently. Writes own simple journal or diary entries independently. Can write several sentences with connected ideas. Refers back using pronouns. Uses connectives such as 'and', 'but', 'because' to link ideas in short texts. Structures used in writing such as word order may reflect some first language features. Uses capital letters appropriately for proper nouns. Uses some more complex punctuation. Supported by class discussion and activities such as modeling, can retell a narrative in writing. Can provide an alternative ending for a story. Shares writing with a partner or a group. Can name all the English letters and knows the sounds they commonly represent. Can present writing appropriately for different audiences or for display using headings, layout and illustrations. May experiment with lettering.

Comment

Writing band 4

Writes in sentences a short story that has a beginning, a middle and an end. Redrafts a piece of writing after a writing conference. Makes corrections to own writing after rereading. Shows an awareness of purpose and audience in choice of vocabulary and style. Uses consistent verb sense. Uses writing to argue, convince or justify. Can write simple descriptions, recounts and procedural text. Works independently when writing but asks for help if needed. Uses a variety of strategies to check spelling. Uses commas to separate items in a list. Can use simple past and future tenses where appropriate. Can use articles correctly. May show confusion over conjunctions and tenses. Uses appropriate verb forms in response to a question that models the form.

Comment

Suggested new indicators

Writing

Reading

Speaking and listening

6 5 4 3 2 1 C B A

WRITING band 4

Nutshell statement

Growing proficiency in English means command of a wider vocabulary and more complex structures to use in writing.

Contexts for observation

- Brainstorming to elicit ideas, new vocabulary, appropriate structures.
- Modeling of narrative writing by teacher. Group reconstructs.
- Guided writing of texts with support from illustrations.
- Post-writing conference

What students may do

Write in sentences a short story that has a beginning, a middle and an end

Make corrections to own writing after rereading

Redraft a piece of writing and make corrections to own writing
After conferencing with teacher

Show an awareness of audience in own writing, in the choice of vocabulary, style and tense

Use writing to argue, convince or justify
Take a point of view on a familiar topic showing some evidence to support this.

Write simple descriptions, recounts and procedural text

Work independently when writing but ask for help if needed

Use commas to separate items in a list

Use simple past and future tenses where appropriate

Use articles incorrectly

Show confusion over conjunctions and tenses

Use appropriate verb forms in response to a question that models the form
'Is Clare coming by bus or by car?'; 'She is coming by car.'

Name .... Arrival date ....

Class .... Age .... Languages spoken at home ....

Writing band 3

Uses a known story form to begin writing. May borrow structures from well-known stories to write own stories. Chooses own topic to write about. Can write a few lines on a topic of interest that has been covered in class. Can write short, factual text independently. Writes own simple journal or diary entries independently. Can write several sentences with connected ideas. Refers back using pronouns. Uses connectives such as 'and', 'but', 'because' to link ideas in short texts. Structures used in writing such as word order may reflect some first language features. Uses capital letters appropriately for proper nouns. Uses some more complex punctuation. Supported by class discussion and activities such as modeling, can retell a narrative in writing. Can provide an alternative ending for a story. Shares writing with a partner or a group. Can name all the English letters and knows the sounds they commonly represent. Can present writing appropriately for different audiences or for display using headings, layout and illustrations. May experiment with lettering.

Comment

Writing band 4

Writes in sentences a short story that has a beginning, a middle and an end. Redrafts a piece of writing after a writing conference. Makes corrections to own writing after rereading. Shows an awareness of purpose and audience in choice of vocabulary and style. Uses consistent verb tense. Uses writing to argue, convince or justify. Can write simple descriptions, recounts and procedural text. Works independently when writing but asks for help if needed. Uses a variety of strategies to check spelling. Uses commas to separate items in a list. Can use simple past and future tenses where appropriate. Can use articles correctly. May show confusion over conjunctions and tenses. Uses appropriate verb forms in response to a question that models the form.

Comment

Writing band 5

Writes for a specific audience. Recognizes different genres. Writes narrative containing direct speech, conversation or dialogue. Can express sustained opinions on topics reflecting prior knowledge. Uses paragraphs to show structure of text. Uses sophisticated link words to connect paragraphs. Uses conventional punctuation and spelling consistently. Can use a range of expressive vocabulary.

Comment

Suggested new indicators

Writing

Reading

Speaking and listening

6 5 4 3 2 1 C B A

WRITING band

5

Contexts for observation

- Pre-writing and writing during writing conferences.
- Modeling of writing genres by teacher, e.g. direct speech and dialogue, writing up a science experiment. Group reconstruction of models.
- Exercises that focus on tools of writing, e.g. punctuation and paragraphing.

What students may do

Write for a specific audience
Peers; school magazine

Recognize different genres
Recount; imaginative story; report

Write narrative containing direct speech, conversation or dialogue

Express sustained opinions on topics reflecting prior knowledge

Use paragraphs to show the structure of the text

Use sophisticated link words to connect planned paragraphs
Although; however; in addition to

Use conventional punctuation and spelling consistently

Use expressive vocabulary
A range of antonyms and synonyms

Writing

Reading

Speaking and listening

A B C 1 2 3 4 **5** 6

Name .... Arrival date ....

Class .... Age .... Languages spoken at home ....

Writing band 4

Writes in sentences a short story that has a beginning, a middle and an end. Redrafts a piece of writing after a writing conference. Makes corrections to own writing after rereading. Shows an awareness of purpose and audience in choice of vocabulary and style. Uses consistent verb tense. Uses writing to argue, convince or justify. Can write simple descriptions, recounts and procedural text. Works independently when writing but asks for help if needed. Uses a variety of strategies to check spelling. Uses commas to separate items in a list. Can use simple past and future tenses where appropriate. Can use articles correctly. May show confusion over conjunctions and tenses. Uses appropriate verb forms in response to a question that models the form.

Comment

Writing band 5

Writes for a specific audience. Recognizes different genres. Writes narrative containing direct speech, conversation or dialogue. Can express sustained opinions on topics reflecting prior knowledge. Uses paragraphs to show structure of text. Uses sophisticated link words to connect paragraphs. Uses conventional punctuation and spelling consistently. Can use a range of expressive vocabulary.

Comment

Writing band 6

Uses varied writing modes successfully for a purpose and audience designated by teacher. Can change a piece of text to suit different audiences. Redrafts to enhance clarity and conciseness. Plans a piece of writing according to appropriate structure, length and style. Can incorporate researched material appropriately into a piece of writing. Uses appropriate verb forms consistently in a piece of writing. Can create an ending to an unfinished piece of writing that maintains a consistency of style and tone. Selects the main ideas from a text, (visual or written) and writes in note form. Using strong teacher support through modeling, can develop ideas logically, using appropriate linking devices throughout a text.

Comment

Suggested new indicators

Writing   Reading   Speaking and listening

A B C 1 2 3 4 5 6

WRITING band 6

Nutshell statement

Writing shows flexibility, adaptability and variety.
Able to participate in mainstream classes.

Contexts for observation

- Pre-writing and post-writing conferences.
- Note-taking exercises, e.g. detailed information from video, lecture by visiting speaker, library research.
- Exercises on incorporation of research into text.
- Writing on a contentious issue.
- Modeling of appropriate genre by teacher. Joint reconstruction of text.

What students may do

Use varied writing modes successfully for purpose and audience designated by teacher
Science report; recipe

Change a piece of text to suit different audiences

Redraft for clarity and conciseness

Plan writing according to appropriate structure, length and style

Incorporate researched material into own writing
By rewriting to match style, tense, etc.

Use appropriate verb forms consistently in writing

Create an ending that maintains consistency of style and tone

Select main ideas from a text and write ideas in note form

Develop ideas logically, using appropriate linking devices, with strong teacher support and modeling

Name .... Arrival date ....

Class .... Age .... Languages spoken at home ....

Writing band 5

Writes for a specific audience. Recognizes different genres. Writes narrative containing direct speech, conversation or dialogue. Can express sustained opinions on topics reflecting prior knowledge. Uses paragraphs to show structure of text. Uses sophisticated link words to connect paragraphs. Uses conventional punctuation and spelling consistently. Can use a range of expressive vocabulary.

Comment

Writing band 6

Uses varied writing modes successfully for a purpose and audience designated by teacher. Can change a piece of text to suit different audiences. Redrafts to enhance clarity and conciseness. Plans a piece of writing according to appropriate structure, length and style. Can incorporate researched material appropriately into a piece of writing. Uses appropriate verb forms consistently in a piece of writing. Can create an ending to an unfinished piece of writing that maintains a consistency of style and tone. Selects the main ideas from a text, (visual or written) and writes in note form. Using strong teacher support through modeling, can develop ideas logically, using appropriate linking devices throughout a text.

Comment

Suggested new indicators

Writing

Reading

Speaking and listening

6 5 4 3 2 1 C B A

Bibliography

Cary, S. 1997. *Second Language Learners*. New York, NY: Stenhouse and the Galef Institute.

Cummins, J. 1981. *Bilingual and Minority Language Children*. Toronto: OISE Press.

Cummins, J. 1989. *Empowering Minority Language Students*. Sacramento, CA: Association for Bilingual Education.

Freeman, D. & Freeman, Y. 1994. *Between Worlds: Access to Second Language Acquisition*. Portsmouth NH: Heinemann.

Griffin, P. & Smith, P. 2000 'Assessing Student's Language Growth: Kirsten's profile' in P. Smith, Ed. *Talking Classrooms: Shaping Children's Learning through Oral Language Instruction*. Newark, DE: International Reading Association.

Griffin, P., Smith, P. & Burrill, L., 1996. *The American Literacy Profile Scales*. Portsmouth, NH: Heinemann.

Griffin, P., Smith, P. & Ridge, N. 2001. *Literacy Profiles in Practice*. Portsmouth, NH: Heinemann.

Krashen, S. 1985. *Inquiries and insights*. Hayward, California: Alemany Press.

Krashen, S. 1994. 'Bilingual Education And Second Language Acquisition Theory,' in *Schooling and Language Minority Students: A Theoretical Framework*, 2nd edn Los Angeles, CA: Evaluation, Dissemination and Assessment Center, California State University.

Krashen, S. & Terrell, T. 1983. *The Natural Approach: Language Acquisition in the Classroom*. Hayward, CA: Alemany Press.

Mead S. K. & Whitmore K. 2000. 'What is in your backpack? Exchanging Funds of Knowledge in an ESL Classroom' in P. Smith, Ed. *Talking Classrooms: Shaping Children's Learning through Oral Language Instruction*. Newark, DE: International Reading Association.

Peyton, J. & Reed, I. 1990. *Dialogue Journal Writing with Non-Native English Speakers: A Handbook for Teachers*. Alexandria, VI: TESOL.

Rivers, W. 1992. Interactive Language Teaching. Cambridge, UK: Cambridge University Press.

Samway, K., Davies & Whang, G. 1996. *Literature Study Circles in a Multicultural Classroom*. York, ME: Stenhouse.

TESOL Publications. ESL standards for Pre-K-12 students, Alexandria, VI: TESOL.

Wallace, C. 1986. *Learning to Read in a Multicultural Society: The Social Context of Second Language Learning*. Oxford, UK: Pergamon Press.

Band Levels

Band	Speaking and listening	Reading	Writing
A		Knows the difference between text and pictures. Knows that text can be supported by illustrations. Relies heavily on illustrations to gain meaning from a text. Can recognize own name in a familiar context in upper or lower case. Can recognize the initial letters of own name in other contexts. Identifies and names some letters. Knows how to handle a book by holding it right way up and turning the pages from front to back. Knows that reading proceeds from left to right and from the top to the bottom of the page. Can join in with or repeat words or phrases during group or individual reading. Shows enjoyment of a well-known story. Chooses to 'read' books for enjoyment.	Draws pictures that relate to an ongoing activity or to tell a story. Knows difference between pictures and print. May write an accompanying text using symbols, letters or copied words. Attributes simple meaning to own writing in English or first language. Uses drawings to support text. Understands that English writing proceeds from left to right and from top to bottom of page. Uses a preferred hand for writing and drawing. Holds pen or pencil using an appropriate grip. Can write own name. May copy words, labels, signs from board, books or charts. Is aware of some sound–symbol relationships. Can recognize some letters. Can copy a simple sentence scribed by teacher from own dictation.
B		Recognizes some isolated words around the room and in known books. Recognizes letters and numerals in texts. Knows there is a difference between first language script and English if the former is non-Roman. Relies on key words for understanding a story read aloud. Relies heavily on extensive teacher support for understanding. Can recognize some signs and labels. Identifies words and spaces in a sentence on request. Can cut up a sentence into words. Can match words. Sequences a known story using pictures. Reads back own writing. Reads sentences scribed by teacher.	Recognizes some words and attempts to reproduce them. Supports own writing by using drawings. Spoken structures and vocabulary reflected in writing. Can form letters appropriately. Leaves spaces between words. Knows difference between upper and lower case letters. Can copy a short passage correctly from the board or a book. Understands some of the terminology of writing. Can finish off short, modeled sentences with some simple personal information. Can draw to support a simple text. Labels own drawings using copied words. Attempts to spell new words. Attempts to write sentences using appropriate spacing between words and ending with a full stop. Asks for words to use in own writing or labeling. Finds some well-known words in charts, books or word banks to use in own writing. Contributes ideas, sentences or words to a class or group story.
C		Recognizes a number of signs and symbols. Demonstrates a sight vocabulary in English comprised of words that have been covered in class activities. Indicates key words in a known story. Can read a well-known text with support. Can track under words when reading. Knows the difference between English and other languages that use the same script. Uses some of the terminology of reading. Understands the function of some punctuation. Demonstrates an understanding of short familiar passages. Can match words to sentences in a known text. Chooses books on topics of interest to take home. Finds words in own dictionary or from class word lists.	Attempts to write letters with consistent size, shape and spacing and in straight lines. May use letter size and color to create a particular feel in a text. Begins to use some punctuation. Can copy a longer passage correctly from the board or a book. Writes simple assessments or reports about self from modeled examples. May write the same texts repeatedly. Uses a known story form to begin writing. Shows an awareness of story from by writing a beginning, a middle and an end in own stories. Can choose own topic to write about, often starting from own drawings. Can write own short texts. Can write for a 'real' task. Includes some words spelt conventionally. Attempts to write unknown words may result in unconventional spelling.

Band	Speaking and listening	Reading	Writing

1

Initiates conversations with mother tongue peers. Interprets and responds appropriately to some non-verbal cues. Repeats the words of other speakers without comprehension. Repeats simple words or phrases appropriately in context. May use first language with teacher or mother tongue peers. Repeats modeled utterances of very short phrases with understanding, usually with a group of other learners.

Knows the difference between text and pictures. Understands that text can be supported by illustrations. Relies heavily on illustrations to gain meaning from a text. Reads own name in full in upper or lower case. Recognizes the initial letters of own name in other contexts. Reads some words around the room or in known books. Can identify some letters and numerals. Identifies words and spaces in a sentence. Recognizes that there is a difference between the graphophonic base of first language and English. Knows how to handle a book. Knows that reading in English proceeds from left to right and from the top to the bottom of the page. Joins in with or repeats words or phrases during a group or individual reading. Shows enjoyment of a well-known story. Chooses to read books for enjoyment.

May initially write in first language. Draws pictures that relate to an ongoing activity or to tell a story. Draws to support a text. Writes own name in full. Completes short sentences with personal information. Completes simple, repetitive modeled sentences. Can copy a sentence scribed by teacher from own dictation. Copies words, labels, signs from the board, books or charts to use in own writing. Copies text correctly from the board or a book. Uses appropriate size, spacing, and letter formation. Is aware of some English sound–symbol relationships.

2

Responds to greetings or to questions in context using facial expressions or gestures. Shows understanding of basic instructions by responding appropriately. Can join in well-rehearsed and well-known songs, rhymes, etc. following the model of peers. May use a memorized expression to gain a specific response or use key words from a formulaic expression. Can answer questions in small groups with a simple word or phrase where the context is clear and the vocabulary well known. Listens for and responds to key words in a sentence. Uses basic intonation to differentiate question and statement. Observes agreed rules for classroom discourse. Recognizes, uses and responds to some informal greetings, introductions and farewells. Speaks at a volume appropriate to the situation.

Relies heavily on key words in a text and on extensive teacher support for understanding. Can recognize some signs, labels, letters and numerals. Identifies and names some letters out of context. Sequences a known story using pictures. Demonstrates a sight vocabulary in English, comprised of words that have been covered in class activities. Reads back own writing, or sentences scribed by teacher from own dictation. Can read a well-known text with support. Can track under words while reading. Knows and uses some of the terminology of reading. Understands the function of some punctuation. Demonstrates an understanding of short familiar passages with a simple, repetitive language pattern. Chooses to look at books independently. Chooses books on topics of interest to take home. Can find words in dictionary or from class word lists. Recognizes the difference between English and other languages that use the same script.

Writes or completes simple sentences from own experiences. May write familiar texts repeatedly, based on modeled repetitive structures. Matches written structures and vocabulary to spoken structures and vocabulary. May use 'and', 'then', 'next' to link ideas in a sentence. Can use repetition and choose vocabulary to add emphasis. Asks the names of things in English to use in own writing. Finds words in charts, books and word banks to use in writing. Can maintain own word banks and topic lists. Finds words from word lists and simple dictionaries. Understands some of the terminology of writing. May use some punctuation to break up ideas. Knows that sentences start with a capital letter. Attempts to spell some new words using knowledge of English graphophonic conventions. Asks for the spelling of words to use in own writing. Contributes ideas, sentences or words to a class or group story.

Band	Speaking and listening	Reading	Writing
3	Can use own simple constructions. May use simple adjectives to describe or add emphasis. Responds to questions from peers or teachers with a single word or phrase. Makes simple requests to satisfy immediate needs, using non-verbal language as well as simple expressions. May initiate communication in a small group. Borrows key words from previous speaker. Shows confidence in familiar class and school routines by responding appropriately to instructions and asking for some clarification. May use structures and copy stress and intonation patterns from familiar repetitive stories, songs and rhymes. Uses some appropriate terminology when requesting. Demonstrates active listening. Enhances speaking by using a variety of non-verbal conventions. Understands that talk can affect other people.	Recognizes and uses visual support to help gain meaning from a text. Uses graphophonic cueing to attack new words. Recognizes individual English words. Modifies intonation when reading to differentiate questions, exclamations or dialogue. Recognizes some different genres. Knows when a story is not yet finished. Concentrates during group reading activities. Reads along with others. Reads supportive texts independently. Recalls important details.	Uses a known story form to begin writing. May borrow structures from well-known stories to write own stories. Chooses own topic to write about. Can write a few lines on a topic of interest that has been covered in class. Can write short, factual text independently. Writes own simple journal or diary entries independently. Can write several sentences with connected ideas. Refers back using pronouns. Uses connectives such as 'and', 'but', 'because' to link ideas in short texts. Structures used in writing such as word order may reflect some first language features. Uses capital letters appropriately for proper nouns. Uses some more complex punctuation. Supported by class discussion and activities such as modeling, can retell a narrative in writing. Can provide an alternative ending for a story. Shares writing with a partner or a group. Can name all the English letters and knows the sounds they commonly represent. Can present writing appropriately for different audiences or for display using headings, layout and illustrations. May experiment with lettering.
4	Can respond to 'Wh' questions in context or to short simple questions. Begins to use 'Wh' question forms, not necessarily accurately. May communicate complex situations using English and non-verbal means. Uses simple English in order to communicate in social situations. Asks what a word means. Uses learned formulaic phrases to meet needs but may not be able to use them correctly in new situations. Has a repertoire of common classroom phrases. Uses the language of play at a basic level. Tries to initiate activities with peers using simple English. Uses some social conventions appropriately. Can express humor and describe feelings.	Chooses to read for interest or to gain specific information. May choose known books from library. Identifies different genres aurally. Reads independently most of the time and with fair understanding. Can read a text for meaning when not all vocabulary is known and be able to identify main points. Interprets maps, graphics and diagrams. Makes a simple critical response to a text or story. Has developed skills in sight organization of discourse, although teacher explanations may be needed for reinforcement. Can read aloud fluently. Pronunciation tends to be correct.	Writes in sentences a short story that has a beginning, a middle and an end. Redrafts a piece of writing after a writing conference. Makes corrections to own writing after rereading. Shows an awareness of purpose and audience in choice of vocabulary and style. Uses consistent verb sense. Uses writing to argue, convince or justify. Can write simple descriptions, recounts and procedural text. Works independently when writing but asks for help if needed. Uses a variety of strategies to check spelling. Uses commas to separate items in a list. Can use simple past and future tenses where appropriate. Can use articles correctly. May show confusion over conjunctions and tenses. Uses appropriate verb forms in response to a question that models the form.
5	Uses most simple 'Wh' questions appropriately. Can transfer known structures to a new situation. Learns English from sources other than the classroom. May ask for names of colors, numbers and interest words. Collects new words from new experiences. Uses key words related to a topic. Can recite a known rhyme, song or chant in an appropriate situation. Makes spontaneous comments in context. Expresses a simple opinion about class texts or events. Relates a simple story or recounts a series of events. May overgeneralize a grammatical rule.	Can comprehend a range of genres at an appropriate level. Reads independently. Understands ESL and mainstream texts at an appropriate level without teacher explanation. Reads for specific information. Can get the gist of a text by skimming and scanning. Can identify main and supporting ideas in texts. Can work out meanings of some unknown words. Comprehends cultural references. Uses supporting evidence from texts to express own opinions. Applies information acquired through reading to other areas.	Writes for a specific audience. Recognizes different genres. Writes narrative containing direct speech, conversation or dialogue. Can express sustained opinions on topics reflecting prior knowledge. Uses paragraphs to show structure of text. Uses sophisticated link words to connect paragraphs. Uses conventional punctuation and spelling consistently. Can use a range of expressive vocabulary.

Band	Speaking and listening	Reading	Writing

6

Talks individually about own experience to adults. Can describe a sequence of events, join ideas using 'and' or 'then'. Describes objects in detail. Uses known vocabulary and knowledge of discourse to promote a conversation. Contributes information in a small group work situation. Expresses own ideas effectively but not necessarily using correct structures to convey meaning. Begins to use pronouns appropriately. Communicates shades of meaning in a limited way. Constructs simple sentences with words in conventional order. Recounts news, events in the immediate past or past experiences. Offers news or information in a whole-class situation. Can retell parts of stories and repeat rhymes, particularly repetitive ones. Can relay simple messages. Uses common time markers. May speak to mother tongue peers in both first language and English. Actively participates in small group and classroom discussions. Can give opinions with some explanations, express likes and dislikes and answer questions in class. Makes suggestions when problem solving in small group.

Uses varied writing modes successfully for a purpose and audience designated by teacher. Can change a piece of text to suit different audiences. Redrafts to enhance clarity and conciseness. Plans a piece of writing according to appropriate structure, length and style. Can incorporate researched material appropriately into a piece of writing. Uses appropriate verb forms consistently in a piece of writing. Can create an ending to an unfinished piece of writing that maintains a consistency of style and tone. Selects the main ideas from a text, (visual or written) and writes in note form. Using strong teacher support through modeling, can develop ideas logically, using appropriate linking devices throughout a text.

7

Can modify spoken language in a variety of situations. Can use extended speech to communicate additional information. Participates in small group discussions. Uses gestures and fillers to sustain a conversation. Retells a story using mostly words from the story. Substitutes words or phrases appropriately in learned expressions. Uses previously learned grammatical structures. Gives specific directions. Can use 'and/but', 'here/there', 'this/that', 'these/those' appropriately. Chooses to explain things in English to other students. Can request or accept opinions or express a choice of option when problem solving in small group. May volunteer answers to teacher questions directed to the whole class. Can talk about own cultural background. Reads or repeats a sentence accurately using appropriate rhythm and intonation.

Band	Speaking and listening	Reading	Writing

8 Uses English in more complex social situations. Asks for repetition, rephrasing or how to say something in English. Can justify and explain. Rephrases questions and answers if they are not understood. Answers questions using 'because'. Responds appropriately to complex questions. Uses new words from class topics or themes in everyday speech. Retells a familiar story using the simple past tense. Expresses own ideas so as to be understood by a mainstream speaker. Is confident enough to give a basic narrative or informative talk. Asks confidently for clarification and definition in conversation. Can self-correct. Engages others in conversation on a range of topics. Expresses an opinion about an issue arising from an abridged or modified text. May elect to work with English-speaking peers rather than own language peers. May correct peers. Experiments with more advanced verb forms. Uses tenses to order events in time. Can recount news or events in the immediate past or past events without assistance. Uses articles with reasonable accuracy. Can join ideas.

9 Speaks fluently. Initiates conversation with other English-speaking people. Seeks information from an unknown person using questions prepared in advance. Initiates and responds to appropriate communication in different registers with people in authority or in subordinate positions. Can initiate complaint to teacher explaining the situation and negotiating a solution. Uses common tag questions naturally in conversation. Is starting to use complex sentences, not necessarily correctly. Can retell an unfamiliar story using own words. Can give a basic talk on how to do a task. Can direct other students by defining a task in a small group discussion.

Nutshell Statements

Band	Speaking and listening	Reading	Writing
A		New to English and new to literacy. Relies heavily on illustrations to support a text. Understands the organization of print in English. Can recognize and name some letters.	New to literacy in English, and perhaps in first language. Relies heavily on pictures and illustrations to communicate.
B		Can recognize some environmental print. Needs extensive support to understand a very simple text. Can read back own writing.	Can recognize some words and attempts to reproduce them. Supports own writing by using drawings. Spoken structures reflected in writing.
C		Has a sign vocabulary in English. Can read a well-known text with support.	Writing shows greater physical control. Repetition of familiar texts. Grasp of story form and own short texts. Some attempts at conventional spelling.
1	Settling into situations where English is the dominant language. Discovering that communication with peers and teachers needs to be conducted in English. Discovering importance of non-verbal communication.	New to English. Relies heavily on illustrations to gain meaning from a text. Recognizes some words in English. Participates in reading activities.	New to literacy in English. May write in first language. Attempts to write in English. Supports writing using illustrations.
2	Communicates simply using a mixture of words, phrases and non-verbal language. Some communication skills transferred from first language to English. Takes part in everyday activities and routines. Models behavior on peers.	Relies heavily on teacher support to establish meaning in a text. Can read a well-known text with support. Knows how to assist own development of literacy in English.	Can write simple sentences. Correlation between written and oral structures and vocabulary. Consciously seeks to increase range of vocabulary and structures for writing.

Band	Speaking and listening	Reading	Writing
3	Communicates simply in English. Takes part in everyday activities and routines. Experiments with the structure of English. Increases knowledge of English by borrowing from other speakers and familiar sources.	Demonstrates various methods of developing reading skills.	Can write for different purposes. Uses a restricted range of structures and vocabulary.
4	Uses English to communicate simple messages. Able to indicate time and tense. Can express simple opinions and ideas.	Able to interpret different sorts of classroom texts. Makes responses to texts. Can recognize word order in familiar texts.	Growing proficiency in English means command of a wider vocabulary and more complex structures to use in writing. Expands vocabulary through many different sources.
5	Gaining a stronger structural control of English through experimentation.	Reads independently. Can perform a range of functions using reading skills.	Writing shows increasing control of structure and genre.
6	Independently communicates experiences with peers and others in a limited way. Sentences contain simple connectives, some pronouns, rudimentary structures and simple descriptors.		Writing shows flexibility, adaptability and variety. Able to participate in mainstream classes.
7	Communicates in English in a variety of situations. Relies heavily on a core of learned vocabulary and structures.		
8	English shows increasing structural and functional control. Sufficient confidence in English to self-correct, correct other ESL speakers and ask questions about language.		
9	Speaks fluently. Uses an increasing variety of structures and subject-specific vocabulary. Can initiate and respond to communication in different registers.		

Blackline masters

Speaking and listening profile rocket

Class .... **School** ....

Teacher .... **Student** ....

9 — Speaks fluently. Uses an increasing variety of structures and subject-specific vocabulary. Can initiate and respond to communication in different registers.

English shows increasing structural and functional control. Sufficient confidence in English to self-correct, correct other ESL speakers and ask questions about language. — **8**

7 — Communicates in English in a variety of situations. Relies heavily on a core of learned vocabulary and structures.

Independently communicates experiences with peers and others in a limited way. Sentences contain simple connectives, some pronouns, rudimentary structures and simple descriptors. — **6**

5 — Expands vocabulary through many different sources. Gaining a stronger structural control of English through experimentation.

Uses English to communicate simple messages. Able to indicate time and tense. Can express simple opinions and ideas. — **4**

3 — Communicates simply in English. Takes part in everyday activities and routines. Experiments with the structure of English. Increases knowledge of English by borrowing from other speakers and familiar sources.

Communicates simply using a mixture of words, phrases and non-verbal language. Some communication skills transferred from first language to English. Takes part in everyday activities and routines. Models behavior on peers. — **2**

1 — Settling into situations where English is the dominant language. Discovering that communication with peers and teachers needs to be conducted in English. Discovering importance of non-verbal communication.

Reading profile rocket

Class .... School ....

Teacher .... Student ....

Reads independently. Can perform a range of functions using reading skills. - - - - - - - - - - **5**

4 - - - - - - - - - Able to interpret different sorts of classroom texts. Makes responses to texts. Can recognize word order in familiar texts.

Demonstrates various methods of developing reading skills. - - - - - - - - - **3**

2 - - - - - - - - - Relies heavily on teacher support to establish meaning in a text. Can read a well-known text with support. Knows how to assist own development of literacy in English.

New to English. Relies heavily on illustrations to gain meaning from a text. Recognizes some words in English. Participates in reading activities. - - - - - - - - - **1**

C - - - - - - - - - Has a sign vocabulary in English. Can read a well-known text with support.

Can recognize some environmental print. Needs extensive support to understand a very simple text. Can read back own writing. - - - - - - - - - **B**

A - - - - - - - - - New to English and new to literacy. Relies heavily on illustrations to support a text. Understands the organization of print in English. Can recognize and name some letters.

Writing profile rocket

6 - - - - - - - - Writing shows flexibility, adaptability and variety. Able to participate in mainstream classes.

Writing shows increasing control of structure and genre. - - - - - - - - - **5**

4 - - - - - - - - Growing proficiency in English means command of a wider vocabulary and more complex structures to use in writing.

Can write for different purposes. Uses a restricted range of structures and vocabulary. - - - - - - - - - **3**

2 - - - - - - - - Can write simple sentences. Correlation between written and oral structures and vocabulary. Consciously seeks to increase range of vocabulary and structures for writing.

New to literacy in English. May write in first language. Attempts to write in English. Supports writing using illustrations. - - - - - - - - - **1**

C - - - - - - - - Writing shows greater physical control. Repetition of familiar texts. Grasp of story form and own short texts. Some attempts at conventional spelling.

Can recognize some words and attempts to reproduce them. Supports own writing by using drawings. Spoken structures reflected in writing. - - - - - - - - - **B**

A - - - - - - - - New to literacy in English, and perhaps in first language. Relies heavily on pictures and illustrations to communicate.

Speaking and listening class profile rocket

Class .... School ....

Teacher ....

Band

Band	Description
9	Speaks fluently. Uses an increasing variety of structures and subject-specific vocabulary. Can initiate and respond to communication in different registers.
8	English shows increasing structural and functional control. Sufficient confidence in English to self-correct, correct other ESL speakers and ask questions about language.
7	Communicates in English in a variety of situations. Relies heavily on a core of learned vocabulary and structures.
6	Independently communicates experiences with peers and others in a limited way. Sentences contain simple connectives, some pronouns, rudimentary structures and simple descriptors.
5	Expands vocabulary through many different sources. Gaining a stronger structural control of English through experimentation.
4	Uses English to communicate simple messages. Able to indicate time and tense. Can express simple opinions and ideas.
3	Communicates simply in English. Takes part in everyday activities and routines. Experiments with the structure of English. Increases knowledge of English by borrowing from other speakers and familiar sources.
2	Communicates simply using a mixture of words, phrases and non-verbal language. Some communication skills transferred from first language to English. Takes part in everyday activities and routines. Models behavior on peers.
1	Settling into situations where English is the dominant language. Discovering that communication with peers and teachers needs to be conducted in English. Discovering importance of non-verbal communication.

Reading class profile rocket

Class .... School ....

Teacher ....

Band

5	Reads independently. Can perform a range of functions using reading skills.	
4	Able to interpret different sorts of classroom texts. Makes responses to texts. Can recognize word order in familiar texts.	
3	Demonstrates various methods of developing reading skills.	
2	Relies heavily on teacher support to establish meaning in a text. Can read a well-known text with support. Knows how to assist own development of literacy in English.	
1	New to English. Relies heavily on illustrations to gain meaning from a text. Recognizes some words in English. Participates in reading activities.	
C	Has a sign vocabulary in English. < None > Can read a well-known text with support.	
B	Can recognize some environmental print. Needs extensive support to understand a very simple text. Can read back own writing.	
A	New to English and new to literacy. Relies heavily on illustrations to support a text. Understands the organization of print in English. Can recognize and name some letters.	

Writing class profile rocket

Class .... School ....

Teacher ....

Band

Band	Description
6	Writing shows flexibility, adaptability and variety. Able to participate in mainstream classes.
5	Writing shows increasing control of structure and genre.
4	Growing proficiency in English means command of a wider vocabulary and more complex structures to use in writing.
3	Can write for different purposes. Uses a restricted range of structures and vocabulary.
2	Can write simple sentences. Correlation between written and oral structures and vocabulary. Consciously seeks to increase range of vocabulary and structures for writing.
1	New to literacy in English. May write in first language. Attempts to write in English. Supports writing using illustrations.
C	Writing shows greater physical control. Repetition of familiar texts. Grasp of story form and own short texts. Some attempts at conventional spelling.
B	Can recognize some words and attempts to reproduce them. Supports own writing by using drawings. Spoken structures reflected in writing.
A	New to literacy in English, and perhaps in first language. Relies heavily on pictures and illustrations to communicate.